CHILDREN'S NEEDS – PARENTING CAPACITY

The impact of parental mental illnes
problem alcohol and drug use, and do   stic
violence on children's developme

CLEAVER, H.,   UNELL, I.   AND   ALDGAT

LONDON: TSO

Published by TSO (The Stationery Office) and available from:

Online
www.tsoshop.co.uk

Mail, Telephone, Fax & E-mail
TSO
PO Box 29, Norwich NR3 1GN
Telephone orders/General enquiries 0870 600 5522
Fax orders: 0870 600 5533
E-mail: customer.services@tso.co.uk
Textphone 0870 240 3701

TSO Shops
123 Kingsway, London WC2B 6PQ
020 7242 6393 Fax 020 7242 6394
16 Arthur Street, Belfast BT1 4GD
028 9023 8451 Fax 028 9023 5401
71 Lothian Road, Edinburgh EH3 9AZ
0870 606 5566 Fax 0870 606 5588

TSO@Blackwell and other Accredited Agents

Published for the Department for Health under licence from the Controller of Her Majesty's Stationery Office.

First published 1999
Ninth Impression 2007

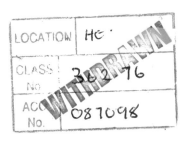
Printed in the United Kingdom for The Stationery Office
5507075 C11 3/07

Table of Contents

Foreword

The Government is firmly committed to improving the lives of our most vulnerable and disadvantaged children. Social Service Departments have an absolutely crucial role to play in improving outcomes for children in need in our communities. To do so effectively, staff at all levels require a good understanding of how to bring about change for children and families and of how to use services most effectively.

In our policy agenda for children set out in Modernising Social Services (1998) and delivered through Quality Protects, the programme for transforming children's social services, we recognise the critical importance of skilled assessment in work with children and families. The Department of Health will shortly be publishing a new framework for assessment, which is grounded in the most recent knowledge from research, policy and practice.

To assist policy makers, managers and practitioners, the Department of Health has commissioned a programme of studies which will inform the new assessment framework. They make an important contribution to the evidence base available for all those working with children and families. This publication by Hedy Cleaver and colleagues at the University of Leicester draws on a wide range of research. It examines how factors such as domestic violence, alcohol and drug misuse and mental illness may impact on children and may effect a parent's capacity to respond to their children's needs.

I hope that this publication will be widely read and that the important messages it contains will find expression in more effective assessment of the needs of children and families. Good assessment, resulting in an effective service response, is vital to ensuring better outcomes for children in need.

John Hutton
Parliamentary Under Secretary of State for Health

Preface

It is probably true to say that for most people childhood is a mixed experience where periods of sadness and loss are balanced with moments of happiness and achievement. Such complexity, however, is rarely represented in the literature of childhood. Indeed, much of the written word in the nineteenth and twentieth centuries depicts childhood in one of two contrasting ways. For example A.A. Milne's (1971) poem 'In the Dark' shows childhood as a golden era where children are loved and nurtured by caring parents. It is a time characterised by innocence, unqualified parental love, irresponsibility, peer friendships and a thirst for adventure and knowledge.

'I've had my supper,
And *had* my supper,
And HAD my supper and all;
I've heard the story
Of Cinderella,
And how she went to the ball;
I've cleaned my teeth,
And I've said my prayers,
And I've cleaned and said them right;
And they've all of them been
And kissed me lots,
They've all of them said "Good-night."

But never far away is the alternative experience, typified by parental desertion, illness, isolation and poverty. Riley (1920) who penned uplifting poems, of perhaps questionable quality, for children during the 1890s paints a much bleaker picture in his poem 'The Happy Little Cripple'.

'I'm thist a little cripple boy, an' never goin' to grow
An' get a great big man at all! – 'cause Aunty told me so.
When I was thist a baby one't, I falled out of the bed
An' got "The Curv'ture of the Spine"– 'at's what the Doctor said.
I never had no Mother nen – fer my Pa runned away
An' dassn't come back here no more – 'cause he was drunk one day
An' stobbed a man in thish-ere town, an' couldn't pay his fine!
An' nen my Ma she died – an' I got "Curv'ture of the Spine!"

Introduction

The present report was commissioned by the Department of Health in recognition of the cumulative evidence from the child protection studies. Its aim is to scrutinise the Department of Health's (1995a) child protection studies and other relevant work, in order to inform children and family social workers about how parental mental illness, problem drinking, drug misuse, or domestic violence may affect the parent(s)' capacity to respond to their children's needs.

The research context

A major theme to emerge from the Child Protection studies, summarised in Child Protection: Messages from Research (Department of Health, 1995), was the high levels of parental mental illness, problem alcohol and drug abuse, and domestic violence in families of children who become involved in the child protection system. Although only a small proportion (15%) of referred cases resulted in the child being registered, many of the families required social work services.

The research evidence showed that parents had problems of their own which adversely affected their ability to respond to the needs of their children. For example, Cleaver and Freeman (1995) found in their study of suspected child abuse that in more than half of cases families were experiencing a number of problems including: mental illness or learning disability, problem drinking and drug use, or domestic violence. In many families these problems had not been identified by the allocated social worker and only came to light during the course of the research. Alternatively, although the issues were known the social worker did not realise the impact they might have on children and other family members.

In addition to identifying issues that could affect parenting the child protection research also revealed that parental problems could influence the process of child protection enquiries (Department of Health, 1995a). A number of key factors were identified. The first of these was parents' anxiety about losing their children. Cleaver and Freeman (1995) noted that in the early stages of a child protection enquiry, families were reluctant to admit to a history of problem drinking or drug use, or a history of mental illness because they assumed it would result in social workers taking more punitive reaction.

For similar reasons families were eager to conceal domestic violence. Farmer and Owen's (1995) research suggests, firstly that hidden domestic violence may account for many mothers' seemingly uncooperative behaviour, and secondly that confronting families with allegations of abuse could compound the mother's vulnerable position. Indeed, case conferences are often ignorant of whether or not children lived in violent families because in the *'face of allegations of mistreatment couples often formed a defensive alliance against the outside agencies...'* (Farmer and Owen 1995 p.79). In fact the authors found that the level of domestic violence (52%) discovered during the research interviews was twice that known at the initial case conference. *'Problems which parents thought would be discrediting were not aired in the early stages – especially those which included domestic violence and alcohol and drug abuse'* (Farmer and Owen, 1995 p.190).

A second factor was that social workers tended to misinterpret parents' behaviour. Social workers were likely to assume guilty or evasive behaviour of parents was related to child abuse. But such behaviour was on occasions found to be the result of parents wanting to keep secret a history of mental illness, illicit drug use, or family problems.

A third factor was that professionals tended to evade frightening confrontations. When social workers were involved with families who had a reputation for violent or bizarre behaviour, suspicions of child abuse were not always as thoroughly enquired into as they might otherwise have been. To confront such families on issues which were likely to result in a violent response was frightening. Research by James (1994) showed that when professionals felt unsupported or must visit alone there was a danger that visiting and child protection enquiries may not always be as thoroughly investigated as they might otherwise be.

A fourth factor was that social workers frequently had a poor understanding of the symptoms of mental illness, problem drinking and drug use, or domestic violence and the consequent impact on the family. Several of the studies argue for greater understanding of parents perspectives (see for example, Cleaver and Freeman, 1995; Farmer and Owen, 1995; Sharland et al, 1996) because unless open and trusting relationships are developed between professionals and parents these issues remained concealed. When this happened it hampered social workers developing alliances with key family members and working in partnership to ensure children could safely remain at home.

Lastly the impact of parental problems on children was not always recognised. Because social workers did not always understand the potential impact of parental mental illness, alcohol or drug problems, or domestic violence on children's development and welfare, children's needs may not be responded to appropriately. *'In some of the conferences family problems which included domestic violence, alcohol abuse and shoplifting were successfully diverted from the agenda'* (Farmer and Owen, 1995 p.172).

Few of the studies explored parental problems in terms of gender and whether this differentially influenced social work intervention. What does become evident is that irrespective of which parent figure was presenting the problem, professionals involved in the child protection process directed their attention to working with mothers. For example, Farmer and Owen (1995) show that in some cases, despite prolonged domestic violence directed from a father figure to the mother and suspicions that the man was also physically abusive to the children, the child protection work focused solely on the mother. However, for many families the possibility of social workers engaging with the father figure was simply not possible because at the time of the child protection enquiry the men were no longer physically present. Cleaver and Freeman's (1995) survey of 583 child protection files found a quarter of children suspected of being abused were cared for by a lone mother.

The legal context

Although many families cope adequately with their problems others, particularly those drawn into the child protection system, would benefit from the assistance of professional agencies to ensure that the hardships they are experiencing do not adversely affect the health and development of their children. Section 17 of the Children Act 1989 takes a developmental approach to the provision of services for children. It places a duty on Local Authorities to provide services under s17 when:

(a)   he is unlikely to achieve or maintain, or to have the opportunity of achieving or maintaining, a reasonable standard of health or development without the provision for him of services by a local authority under part 111;

(b)   his health or development is likely to be significantly impaired, or further impaired, without the provision for him of such services; or

(c)   he is disabled.

The Children Act 1989 is founded on the assumption that it is generally best for children to grow up within their own family and that most parents want to carrry out their parental responsibilities autonomously. It also recognises that it is normal for families to have problems from time to time and to turn to the State for help. At these times parents may have needs in their own right that impact on their children's well-being.

> *'Parents are individuals with needs of their own. Even though services may be offered primarily on behalf of their children, parents are entitled to help and consideration in their own right. ...Their parenting capacity may be limited temporarily or permanently by poverty, racism, poor housing or unemployment or by personal or marital problems, sensory or physical disability, mental illness or past life experiences...'* (Department of Health, 1991, p.8.)

Research on child protection, family support and 'looked after' children has all suggested that many of the families who are known to social services are subject to multiple stressors (Bebbington and Miles, 1989; Department of Health, 1995a; Aldgate and Tunstill, 1995; Tunstill and Aldgate, forthcoming; Packman and Hall 1998).

Any assessment of families has to take into acount the complexity of stressors they may be experiencing. Professionals need assistance in deciding what services are required to support families in order to safeguard and promote the welfare of their children. One attempt to identify the services that might be needed is Cleaver and Freeman's (1995) typology of families. This enables social workers to identify the range, type and duration of services required to support the family and ensure the safety and welfare of the children. This has more general application where the parental problems place children and families in need of services under s17. Three categories in this typology are particularly relevant:

- **Multi-problem families** are well known to the welfare and control agencies and experience a range of problems, many of which are chronic. Problems may include: ill health, poor housing, long-term unemployment, domestic violence, drunkenness, drug abuse, and financial and social incompetence.

- **Specific problem families** are rarely known to agencies and come to their attention because of a specific issue, for example parental mental illness. Families are not confined to any social class and, on the surface, their lives may appear quite ordered.

- **Acutely distressed families** normally cope but an accumulation of events overwhelmed their resources. They *tend to be composed of a single or poorly-supported and immature parents or others who are physically ill or disabled.* (Cleaver and Freeman, 1995, p.52).

What is striking about this typology and the profiles of families from research on family support (see Aldgate and Bradley in press;

Thoburn et al, forthcoming) is their similarity. The typologies make a clear distinction between families who have many chronic problems which require long term, multi-service input and those who normally cope well but have been recently overwhelmed by problems.

One of the difficulties in addressing the problems experienced by these families is that they require a service approach which enables adults' and children's services to collaborate. This approach would ensure that not only are parents recognised as having needs in their own right, but the impact of those needs on children becomes part of a multi-agency service response.

In spite of Children's Services Plans which have been developed to address children's multi-faceted needs, there are continuing problems in formal collaboration between services for adults and children. This has come about due to a variety of professional, legislative and structural reasons. These create boundaries around adults' and children's services which increases the difficulty of securing an holistic approach to the needs of the family. It remains to be seen whether this can be mitigated by the present government's objectives for Health and Social Services (Department of Health, 1998).

The structure of the book

In considering how parental mental illness, problem drinking, drug misuse, or domestic violence may affect the child, a developmental model is applied. Research findings are desegregated through applying the developmental dimensions produced to assess and measure outcomes for children in the public care system (Department of Health, 1995b). There are seven developmental dimensions: health, education, identity, family and social relationships, social presentation, emotional and behavioural development and self care skills.

Because the impact on the child of parental problems will depend on a variety of factors including the child's age and developmental stage, similar age bands to those used in the Looking After Children materials are applied (Ward, 1995).

For example, with regard to the educational development of children aged 3–4 years, it is important to identify when, for example, the parents' mental illness, or problem drinking and drug use, or domestic violence, substantially restricts the child's access to stimulating toys, drawing or writing material and books, or prevents parents spending sufficient time talking, reading or playing with their children.

Alternatively, assessing the impact of these same parental issues on the education of young adolescents aged 10–14 years needs to focus on different themes – such as school attendance and the child's involvement in other learning activities such as sport, music or hobbies.

Within each dimension and for each age group evidence is used to highlight both the adverse impact on children and the factors which act as protectors; such as strategies children use to cope with stressful family situations, and the use of wider family and community resources.

The information is presented under 5 sections:

Part one questions whether concern is justified, and explores the problems of definition and prevalence.

Part two explores the ways mental illness, problem drug use including alcohol, or domestic violence affect parents.

Part three identifies which children are vulnerable.

Part four discusses the impact of parental mental illness, problem drinking/drug use or domestic violence on child development. This is done in the context of the Looking After Children dimensions (Ward, 1995).

Part five discusses the implication of the report's findings for policy and practice.

Part one:

Is concern justified – problems of definition and prevalence

In seeking to understand whether the present concerns over parental mental illness, problem alcohol and drug use, or domestic violence is justified, this section examines the following issues:

- Problems with terminology
- The prevalence of parental mental illness
- The prevalence of parents with a drink problem
- The prevalence of parents with a drug problem
- The prevalence of domestic violence.

Problems with terminology

Understanding the rates of parental mental illness, problem drug use including alcohol, or domestic violence is difficult because different research studies use different terms and there are no or few definitions provided. For example, in the Department of Health's 1995 studies on child protection (Department of Health, 1995a) it is unclear whether Sharland et al's (1996) parents who have 'relationship problems' are a similar group to Thoburn et al's (1995) parents who are in 'marital conflict', or Farmer and Owen's (1995) families with 'domestic violence'.

In discussing the impact of these issues on families the term 'parent' is used in a generic way to refer to any adult responsible for parenting the children. Thus the mentally ill 'mother' could be the birth mother, step mother, foster mother, father's live-in girl friend, or female relative who is bringing up the child.

In scrutinising the literature on mental illness, problem alcohol and drug use, or domestic violence this report has been guided in the use of terms by the following policy and practice documents.

Mental illness

Clinical studies of adults generally define mental illness either by using the European system: ICD-10 classification of mental illness and behavioural disorders (World Health Organisation, 1992) or the U.S. classification: Diagnostic and Statistical Manual of Mental Disorders (American Psychiatric Association, 1994). Unfortunately, the quality of information from community based records may preclude such a precise diagnosis. In addition, there continues to be considerable dispute over whether 'personality disorder' is a psychiatric illness as such or merely a description of relationship problems (see for example Falkov, 1997; Reder and Duncan, 1997). But because *'personality dysfunction has been repeatedly described in anecdotal case reports, clinical studies and surveys of the parents of maltreated children'* (Falkov, 1997, p.42) it was thought that to omit it in a study of the impact on children of parental problems would be remiss.

Problem drinking

The 1997 report by Alcohol Concern (Brisby et al, 1997, p.7) defines problem drinking as *'consumption above 35 units a week for women and 50 units a week for men'*. But basing problem drinking only on how much is consumed weekly may lead to problems being missed, because even relatively light drinking i.e. under 21 units of alcohol a week for men, can be problematic if the alcohol is consumed all at one time. Similarly, the heavy use of some drugs, like methadone, may be less debilitating for parents than problematic use of legal drugs such as alcohol.

Problem drug use

With regard to problem drug use this report follows the lead taken by the Standing Conference on Drug Abuse (1997). Problem drug use is defined in terms of the negative effects that usage has on families, i.e. social, financial, relationship, psychological, physical or legal problems.

Domestic violence

When considering domestic violence the following definition used by the Crown Prosecution Service was found to be helpful:

> *Any form of physical, sexual or emotional abuse which takes place within the context of a close relationship. In most cases, the relationships will be between partners (married, co-habiting or otherwise) or ex-partners.*

This definition does not confine itself to physical or sexual assaults but includes other forms of domestic violence such as harassment, mental violence, restrictions on liberties, isolation, threats of violence, deprivation and damage or loss of property (Department of Health, 1997b). In addition, it needs to be noted that domestic violence recognises few boundaries. For example research on female victims of domestic violence reports that *'Violence against women is the most demo-*

cratic of all crimes, it crosses all religious, class and race barriers' (Women's Aid, 1995).

Prevalence

One of the first questions to address is how prevalent these issues are in families with dependant children. Many adults have times when they suffer from anxiety or depression, have relationships with partners which are unstable, drink alcohol and increasing numbers have used drugs, both licit and illicit, but this does not mean they are poor parents. It is the extremity or combination of these situations, particularly the association with violence, which may impair children's health and development.

Unfortunately the ability to accurately gauge the extent of parental mental illness, problem alcohol/drug use or domestic violence is hampered not only by problems of terminology but also because prevalence depends upon the population group being studied. For example, community based samples such as the household survey carried out by OPCS (1996) will be more representative than research which focuses on specific groups, such as hospital patients, outpatients, or those who attend clinics or courts. However, the severity of the condition under study is likely to be much greater in specific sample groups as is the co-existence of a variety of different problems. But regardless of the type of sample group under consideration, any generalisations to samples beyond that being studied should be made with considerable caution.

The following section explores in turn the existing evidence on the prevalence of parental mental illness, problem drinking and drug use, or domestic violence. Two sources are examined: general population studies and child protection research.

Prevalence of parental mental illness: general population studies

There is wide variation in the morbidity of different types of mental illness. For example the OPCS (1996) household survey shows that 160 per thousand of the adult population experienced a neurotic disorder during the survey week. In contrast, the prevalence of functional psychoses is much lower – a rate of only 4 per thousand of the adult population in the twelve months prior to the study date. An earlier study of schizophrenia, based in a single health authority, shows a similar level of morbidity (Bamrah et al, 1991).

Some forms of mental illness are more prevalent than others and the following table compares the rate of different types of mental illness within the general population derived from community based studies.

Table 1: **Prevalence of mental illness amongst adults in the general population**

Type of mental illness	Rate	Source of data
Schizophrenia	0.6–1.0%	Bamrah, 1991
Depression	5.0%	Kandal et al, 1991
Personality disorders	10.0%	Zimmerman and Coryell, 1990
Anxiety disorders	10–30%	Kandal et al, 1991

These studies provide no information on what proportion of sufferers are also parents responsible for caring for children. The OPCS (1996) survey, which breaks down the data by the type of family unit, shows psychiatric morbidity to be associated with family characteristics. Couples living with child(ren) have a greater morbidity for both neurotic disorder (155 per thousand) and functional psychoses (4 per thousand) than couples without children (134 per thousand for neurotic disorder and 2 per thousand for functional psychoses). Similarly, a lone parent and child(ren) has a higher rate for neurotic disorder than a single adult alone without children (281 per thousand compared to 209 per thousand).

Children are more vulnerable when living with a lone parent who suffers from mental illness, because when the parent is experiencing difficulties there is no other caring adult living in the home to take on the parenting role. The OPCS (1996) data shows a higher rate of mental illness for lone parents than for adults living as a couple with children.

Table 2: **The prevalence of mental illness amongst parents in the general population**

Type of mental illness	Couple and child(ren)	Lone parent and child(ren)
Neurotic disorders	15.5%	28%
Functional psychoses	0.4%	1.1%

Information on the prevalence of parental mental illness can also be found in studies which focus on adult mental health services. Falkov examines the evidence and suggests '*that a substantial proportion (at least*

20%, probably a third and in some cases up to 50%) of adults known to mental health services have children …' (Falkov forthcoming).

Parental mental illness: issues of gender, culture and class

Research on the prevalence and impact on children of paternal mental illness is sparse. What is clear is that men, living either as a couple with children or in a lone parent situation, have a lower rate of neurotic disorder and functional psychoses than do women in similar situations (OPCS, 1996).

A considerable body of work records the rate of mental illness in mothers. Somewhat surprising is that the prevalence of maternal mental illness appears to vary from country to country. For example, in America as many as 25–39% of women suffer depression following childbirth (Bettes, 1988). British studies place the figure at around 10% (O'Hara et al, 1984; Cooper et al, 1988). One might question whether the variance in reported rates of mental illness is due to real differences in prevalence, in how mental illness manifests itself, or in methods of assessment and recording.

Research into the impact of race, class and culture suggests a further complicating factor in gauging prevalence. Mental illness is linked to social class. A scrutiny of the adult population shows social class V (unskilled, manual occupations) to have the highest rates of neurotic disorder and functional psychoses (OPCS, 1996). The impact of class is exacerbated when adults are parents caring for children. *'… among those with children at home, working-class women were four times more likely to suffer from a definite psychiatric disorder'* than comparable middle-class women (Brown and Harris, 1978, p.278).

Vulnerability to mental disorders may be the result of adverse life events such as poverty, sexism or racism and other forms of social disadvantage. Of particular significance are those involving long-term threat (Brown and Harris, 1978; Sheppard, 1993).

The picture is further clouded because mental illness is perceived differently by different cultural groups (Rack, 1982; NSPCC, 1997a). For example, the literature seems to suggest that in some south Asian cultures mental illness is expressed in terms of physiological ailments. As a result symptoms may be reported as problems requiring medical rather than psychiatric services (Rack, 1982). Likewise, in many cultures outside the Western world schizophrenia is interpreted as a possession of the sufferer by malevolent spirits and the services of priests rather than doctors are sought (Coulter, 1973; Littlewood and Lipsedge, 1989).

This cumulative body of evidence shows the difficulties in assessing prevalence but at the same time suggests that a considerable number of children are living in families where at least one parent is suffering from a mental illness.

Prevalence of parental mental illness: child protection studies

An alternative source of information on rates of parental mental illness, problem alcohol or drug use, or domestic violence, is to examine data from research on child protection. Indeed, many of the recently published Department of Health research studies into child protection (summarised in Department of Health, 1995a) indicate that a significant proportion of children who come into the child protection system are from families where these issues are present. For example, Cleaver and Freeman (1995) found in their study of suspected child abuse that 'multi-problem' families (where more than one of these issues was present) made up 43% of cases. Moreover, the children from these 'multi problem' families were 3 times more likely to be re-abused than children from families with fewer stressors.

This profile of families having multiple problems was also shown by Gibbons et al (1995a) in their large scale study of children referred to the child protection system. As with previous research (see for example Rutter and Quinton, 1984, Birtchnell and Kennard, 1983) children were particularly vulnerable when mental illness or problem alcohol use occurred in conjunction with domestic violence.

In studies which focus on all types of child abuse, the prevalence of identified mental illness increases with the level of enquiry. At the referral stage prevalence is low. Gibbons et al (1995a) found that in 13% of all child protection referrals parental mental illness was recorded.

Once a first enquiry interview has been undertaken prevalence increases. Cleaver and Freeman (1995) identified mental illness in some 20% of cases (unpublished material).

When cases come under greater scrutiny and a child protection conference is held, prevalence increases once again. Parental mental illness was identified in a quarter of cases which were conferenced (Farmer and Owen, 1995).

There is a further rise in prevalence for children involved in care proceedings. Hunt et al (forthcoming) found that parental mental illness was recorded in 42% of cases where children were the subject of care proceedings.

Early research on child murder recorded particularly high rates of maternal mental illness. Resnich's (1969) review of 131 cases of parental child murder identified 71% of mothers as depressed and Gibson's (1975) study of maternal filicide noted 90% of mothers as having a psychiatric disorder. More recent research into extreme cases of child abuse tempers these findings. Falkov's (1996) study of fatal child abuse found at least a third of parents had a psychiatric disorder, a similar rate to that noted by d'Orban (1979). The focus on mothers, given by much of the child protection research, might suggest that they are more prone to killing their children. However, Stroud's (1997) review shows that filicide is not just carried out by mothers, fathers are just as likely to murder their child as are mothers.

Parental mental illness and type of child abuse

There is a further important issue to be considered; the possible association between parental mental illness and type of child abuse. A search of the literature failed to uncover any work which specifically explores this link. Studies focusing on specific types of child abuse suggest parental mental illness is associated with emotional or sexual abuse. For example, when children are registered as emotionally abused, parental mental illness was recorded in 31% of cases (Glaser et al, 1997).

Research on child sexual abuse suggests a greater association with parental mental illness. Sharland et al's (1996) study of child sexual abuse found 71% of families, where there were suspicions of abuse, were in a 'poor psychological state' (using the General Health Questionnaire) and there was a further increase when suspicions were confirmed. These findings are in line with Monck et al's (1996) study of families attending a specialised treatment and assessment day clinic for child sexual abuse. They found 86% of mothers (assessed using the General Health Questionnaire) showed symptoms of depression or anxiety and, for a considerable proportion, the symptoms had been of long duration.

Caution, however, must be exercised in relation to these findings because studies of physical abuse and neglect have tended not to use standardised measures of mental health and one is not comparing like with like.

Prevalence of parents with a drink problem: general population studies

Alcohol is a common feature of many people's lives in the United Kingdom. Estimates from Alcohol Concern (House of Commons, 1991) suggest about 90% of adults drink alcohol. Problematic alcohol use is much less common. The Lord President's Report estimated that some 1.4 million people in the UK drink harmfully, that is 50 units of alcohol a week for men and 35 units of alcohol a week for women (House of Commons, 1991). In addition to problems being caused by regular or habitual excessive drinking, problems can be caused by binge drinking or occasional intoxication or unsafe drinking, for example drinking before driving (Velleman, 1993).

The OPCS (1996) household survey gives data on the rate of alcohol dependence by type of family unit. Unlike mental illness the rate of alcohol dependence for couples living together is similar (27 per thousand) irrespective of whether or not they have dependant children. Lone parents show a higher rate (38 per thousand) than found for couples with children, although this is significantly lower than that for single adults living alone (102 per thousand). These findings reflect those for mental illness and suggest that children living with a lone parent are more vulnerable to the impact of parental drinking than children in households where adults live as a couple.

Further information comes from Brisby et al (1997) who attempts to calculate how many children are currently living in families where parental alcohol consumption is a problem. Their admitted approximate calculation indicates some 7% of parents are drinking at harmful levels. Through extrapolating from census data they suggest that this indicates *'some 800,000 children in England and Wales, 85,000 children in Scotland and something under 35,000 children in Northern Ireland are living in a family where a parent has an alcohol problem'* (Brisby et al, 1997, p.7). Not all of these children will suffer significant harm (Rydelius, 1997). Research suggests that if parental problem drinking is not associated with violence, children are no more likely to develop problems than any other child (Velleman and Orford, 1993).

Problem drinking: issues of gender, culture and class

The issue of gender in parental drinking was highlighted by the work of ChildLine (1997). An analysis of all calls received in the year 1 April 1995 to 31 March 1996 shows 3,255 children talked about their parents' problematic drinking. The majority (57%) identified a male figure (fathers, step fathers, or mother's boyfriend) as the problem drinker. Mothers also featured: a third (33%) of children mentioned their mother or mother figure had an alcohol problem. Seven per cent indicated both parents had a drink problem.

Gender also has an impact on drinking patterns. Men from social class V are the heaviest drinkers amongst men. However women from social class V are significantly under the average for women's drinking as a whole (The Royal College of Physicians, 1991).

Culture may also influence drinking patterns. For example, cultures in which religious beliefs eschew alcohol are likely to result in lower rates of problem drinking than those cultures where alcohol is freely available. *'The rate of alcohol abuse in Muslim families is extremely low, as it is in first generation Sikh families'* (Royal College of Physicians, 1995, p.16).

Prevalence of parents with a drug problem: general population studies

Drug use is not as common as drinking alcohol. Nevertheless, Leitner et al (1993) report that at least half the adult population aged 19–59 have tried illicit drugs. The OPCS (1996) survey also gives data on the prevalence of drug dependence in the general population. This data shows a similar pattern to that found for alcohol dependence. Households where adults live as a couple have a low rate of drug dependence (7 per thousand for couples without children and 9 per thousand when there is a child present). As with alcohol dependence a higher rate of drug dependence is found amongst lone parents (24 per thousand). Nonetheless, this rate is less than half that recorded for single adults living without children (52 per thousand). Again the vulnerability of children to the impact of parental drug use, of living with a lone parent, compared to those who live with two caring adults, is revealed.

Information on the use of specific types of illicit drugs amongst parents caring for dependant children is particularly sparse. Data published by the Trent Drug Misuse Database (1998) shows 3,490 individuals sought agency help for drug problems during the year 1996–1997, of whom more than 7 out of 10 reported their main drug as an opiate, such as Heroin.

Practically a fifth (19.4%) of all problem drug users in the Trent region were known to have dependant children (aged under 18), most (90%) of whom lived at home. On average parents who were problem drug users had 2.0 children, thus approximately 1,354 children in the Trent area lived with a family where a parent was a problem drug user. Only 29 parents (4%) admitted to being in contact with social services departments, though it is likely that many more were but the information was not recorded with the treatment agency.

The statistical information from the Trent Drug Misuse Database is certainly an under-estimation of the number of children of parents coming for help within Trent Region. Many clients of agencies were not asked if they had dependant children or, when they were, the information was not recorded.

There is little or no U.K. research into the rate of cocaine crack use amongst social service clients. Although great caution should be used in transferring findings from research which is not U.K. based, Canadian research (Leslie, 1993) suggests that the problem may be considerable. These findings suggest that in some 25% of active cases, from one social work agency, at least one parent had a drug problem. When cocaine crack was the main drug used, the mother was most often identified as the user.

Prevalence of parents with a drink or drug problem: child protection studies

Data from child protection studies shows a similar association to that found for mental illness. The increasing level of social work intervention was linked with an increasing rate of parental problem alcohol or drug use.

At the referral stage 20% of families were found to have a history of drug or alcohol problems (see for example Gibbons et al, 1995a; NSPCC, 1997b).

When families are interviewed because of suspicions about child abuse the rate increases to 25% (Cleaver and Freeman, 1995).

In English based research a prevalence of 25% was found for the next stage of enquiry – when families attended a child protection conference (Thoburn et al, 1995; Farmer and Owen, 1995). However, research based in Wales found a much higher rate, heavy drinking or intoxication was a factor in some 60% of cases at the child protection conference stage (quoted in Brisby et al, 1997).

Finally, the figure was found to rise to 70% when children were the subject of court orders (Rickford, 1996).

Problem drinking or drug misuse and the type of child abuse

As with mental illness, research which explores parents' problem drinking and drug misuse indicates an association with particular types of child abuse. For example, parental problem drinking is associated with the physical abuse of children (Famularo et al, 1992). But who is doing the drinking may also be relevant. Although alcohol was cited in 20% of cases when children reported physical abuse at the hands of their father, this was not the case when mothers drank excessively. Maternal problem drinking was more frequently linked to child neglect. '*One third of calls reporting neglect include a parent abusing drugs or alcohol. This was most often the mother. Alcohol was mentioned in two of three of these cases*' (NSPCC 1997b, p.35).

In contrast, research which explores the association between parental problem drug misuse and child abuse suggests cocaine addiction is associated with the sexual abuse of children (Famularo et al, 1992).

As with parental mental illness, no systematic research into the association between problem drinking or drug misuse and child abuse exists. Further work is required to test whether there are causal links and specific mechanisms between parental problem drinking and various forms of child abuse.

Prevalence of domestic violence: general population studies

There are serious problems in accurately identifying the prevalence of domestic violence. The scale of the problem is likely to be greater than official statistics suggest because people are reluctant to reveal domestic violence and hesitant about seeking help. Dominy and Radford's (1996) study of 484 women victims of domestic violence found only one in three had previously told anyone of their experiences, a figure which reflects earlier findings by Dobash and Dobash (1980).

There are signs that the reporting of domestic violence has increased. Since 1981, the largest increase in violent crime has been the reporting of incidents of domestic violence and the British Crime Survey (1996) identified almost a million incidents in England and Wales.

In most recorded instances (90–95% of cases) women are the victims and men perpetrate the violence (Dobash and Dobash, 1992). Research suggests domestic violence is experienced by between 18 to 30% of women. A randomly selected sample of 1,000 men and women living in North London found that 1 in 4 women had been subject to domestic violence (Mooney, 1994). A similar level (25%) of domestic violence was reported in a much larger Canadian telephone survey involving a random sample of 12,300 women (Statistics Canada, 1993). Also in line with these trends is the Irish data which found 18% of women had been subjected to violence by an intimate partner at some stage of their lives (Office of the Tanaiste, 1997).

Although we have increasing information about prevalence, the degree of the violence is less well documented. Nevertheless, it is very disturbing to discover 18% of all injuries seen in hospital emergency rooms are the result of domestic violence (Stark et al, 1979) and on average two women per week are killed in England and Wales by partners or former partners (Home Office, 1994).

The Women's Aid Federation of England (WAFE), which is a national co-ordinating organisation for refuge groups, also offers additional information on the extent of domestic violence perpetrated against women. They show that 45,000 women and children were given accommodation in the year 1992–3, a figure that rose to over 63,000 in 1996–7 (Women's Aid Federation Annual Survey, 1993–4 and 1996–7). Domestic violence may result in children moving away from home. Data from WAFE shows that children represent over two-thirds of the refuge population (Ball quoted in Saunders, 1994; Women's Aid Federation, 1991 and 1993). Domestic violence is also shown to be the most common cause of homelessness among women caring for school-age children (Thomas and Niner, 1989). When this occurs the consequences for children can be far reaching. To have to leave home may result in a change of school and a disruption of friendships and social contacts.

Research has generally focused on violence perpetrated by male partners on women. Studies of violence by women against male partners or relationships which are mutually violent are unusual. As a result, although there is a growing body of research which explores domestic violence from the women's perspective, the experiences of male victims remain largely unknown (Cook, 1997). Moffitt and Caspi's (1998) research which shows that partner violence is not role specific, highlights the ignorance which surrounds this aspect of domestic violence. Recent research suggests that mutual combat may be the norm in many violent households, but that attacks by women tend only to be reported when they are very dangerous or result in serious injury (Cook, 1997). There is little research on the impact on children of mutual violence or violence perpetrated by women. However, regardless of the gender of the perpetrator, witnessing adults hitting, pushing or shoving one another, even if no injuries occur, gives to children the message that violence is acceptable behaviour.

Prevalence of domestic violence: child protection studies

As with mental illness and parental alcohol and drug misuse, research which focuses on the child reveals a similar link between the level of child abuse concerns and the known prevalence of domestic violence.

Gibbons et al's (1995a) study of all child protection referrals noted that domestic violence occurred in approximately a quarter (27%) of cases.

At the point when concern warranted a visit to the family the rate of domestic violence rose to 40% (Cleaver and Freeman, 1995).

Thoburn et al (1995) suggest a figure of 35% at the child protection conference stage, but acknowledge that much violence may be hidden, *'the amount of present and past marital conflict is almost certainly underestimated'* (Thoburn et al, 1995, p.38). This claim is substantiated by Farmer and Owen (1995) who found a similar rate of reporting by social workers at the child protection conference stage, although subsequent research interviews with families revealed the higher rate of 52%. This is in line with figures from the NSPCC (1997b), which estimated that domestic violence was present in over half (55%) of child protection cases they had dealt with.

Finally, the level remains fairly constant when children are the subject of care proceedings. Hunt et al (forthcoming) found that domestic violence was an issue in 51% of cases coming to court.

Domestic violence and the type of child abuse

There is considerable evidence that *'adult partners who are violent toward each other are also at increased risk of abusing their children'* (Moffitt and Caspi, 1998, p.137; Gibbons et al, 1995b). The risk of child abuse is shown to be between three and nine times greater in homes where the adult partners hit each other (Moffitt and Caspi, 1998).

Additional evidence for a link between domestic violence and physical child abuse comes from feminist research. An American study of 'wife beating', using a voluntary sample of 1,000 women, found *'wife beaters abused children in 70% of families where children were present'* (Bowker et al, 1988, p.162). In contrast, the NCH (1994) study of children living with domestic violence found only 27% of children were reported by the mother as 'hit or abused'. The large disparity between these findings may be deceptive. The authors suggest the figure of 27% may under-represent the prevalence of physical child abuse because mothers are reluctant to disclose the abuse or are ignorant of it. In another study less than half the mothers (44%) reported that their violent partners 'didn't touch the children' (NCH, 1994, p.31).

Summary of the evidence for a link between parental problems and child abuse

A review of the research literature has revealed a similar pattern for the known prevalence of parental mental illness, problem alcohol and drug use and domestic violence. When families come to the attention of social work services, because of concerns about the children, the rate of parental problems shows a considerable increase from that found in the general population. Moreover, based on the data from a number of different research studies, Table 3 shows the prevalence continues to rise with the seriousness of the child protection enquiry.

Table 3: **The relationship between the rate of recorded parental problems and the level of social work intervention.**

Parental problems	Referral stage	First enquiry	Child protection conference	Care proceedings	Serious injury or death
	%	%	%	%	%
Mental illness	13	20	25	42	33–90
Alcohol/ drugs	20	25	25–60	70	
Domestic violence	27	40	35–55	51	

Caution is needed in interpreting this data because we do not know whether the increase reflects a true picture of what is happening or simply that parents' problems had not been recognised or recorded at an earlier stage in the assessment procedure.

To sum up

- Prevalence is difficult to assess because different studies use different terms. For example, it is not clear whether 'domestic violence' is synonymous with 'marital conflict'.
- The information concerning the prevalence of mental illness, problem alcohol/drug use, or domestic violence in families with dependant children is incomplete.

- Children are most vulnerable when parental mental illness or problem alcohol and drug use coexist with domestic violence.

- The data from child protection research suggests that the prevalence of reported parental mental illness, problem drug use including alcohol, or domestic violence increases incrementally as the investigation progresses.

Part two:

The ways mental illness, problem alcohol/drug use or domestic violence effect parents

Having looked at the prevalence of adult mental illness, problem drinking and drug misuse or domestic violence, it is important to explore the experiences of sufferers and how these issues can effect parenting.

To suggest that all parents who suffer from mental illness, problem alcohol/drug use or domestic violence present a danger to their children is misleading. Indeed, much research indicates that in isolation problem alcohol/drug use or mental illness of a parent presents little risk of significant harm to children. Rutter and Quinton (1984) in their four year follow-up study of children, found two thirds of those in families where there was parental mental illness suffered no long-term behavioural or emotional difficulties.

Furthermore, there is considerable evidence that many, if not most, children of parents with problem alcohol and drug use eventually 'outgrow' their troubled childhood and develop into balanced, productive adults and parents (Werner, 1986; Orford and Velleman, 1990; Tweed, 1991; Avis, 1993). The best predictor of adverse long-term effects on children is the co-existance of mental illness or problem drinking with family disharmony. When families remain cohesive and harmonious, the children generally grow up relatively unharmed (see Quinton and Rutter, 1985 for mental illness; Velleman, 1993 for problem drinking).

Similarly, general population studies found that '*Although marital disharmony increases the risk to children of demonstrating psychiatric disturbance, most children in disharmonious homes do not show problems*' (Jenkins and Smith, 1990, p.60).

While caution is needed in making assumptions about the impact on children of parental mental illness, problem alcohol or drug use or domestic violence, if the issues coexist the risk to the children increases considerably. There is substantial independent evidence from research into both parental mental illness and problem alcohol or drug use, that the combination of issues, particularly the link with domestic violence, is potentially dangerous for children (in relation to alcohol see for example, Billings et al, 1979; Velleman and Orford, 1993; Brisby et al, 1997; for mental illness see Rutter and Quinton, 1984; Falkov, 1996).

Given these two caveats the next step is to understand how parental mental illness, problem alcohol or drug use, or domestic violence affect the behaviour of adults. Only by knowing the possible behavioural outcomes for parents with these kinds of problems can we begin to identify the impact which this may have on children. It is also important to understand both the experience of sufferers and the consequences for other aspects of their lives which can influence parenting and consequently the ability to respond to their children's needs.

There are two major issues: the psychological impact; and the social consequences of parental mental illness, problematic alcohol and drug use, or domestic violence. The psychological impact is explored separately for each issue before dealing more generally with the possible social consequences.

The physical and psychological impact of mental illness

The following section attempts to give details of the sufferer's experience of the most common forms of mental illness, although part of the section will inevitably be describing symptoms perceived by both patients and clinicians. Nevertheless, this is an attempt to emphasise the impact of symptoms on the daily lives of parents.

Schizophrenia

Schizophrenia is an episodic illness. With the onset of the illness sufferers often withdraw from their friends and colleagues and spend increasing amounts of time alone. They experience difficulties in functioning, frequently neglect their personal hygiene, behave in an odd manner, are plagued by strange ideas and find their emotions become blunted. During a schizophrenic episode the sufferer loses contact with objective reality and becomes increasingly preoccupied with his or her inner, private life. Schizophrenics by definition (see Kandal et al, 1991) experience one or more of the following symptoms:

1. Bizarre delusions (for example, they feel persecuted and believe their feelings, thoughts and actions are controlled by an outside force).
2. Prominent hallucinations, usually auditory (for example, voices comment on everything they do).
3. Disordered memory and thoughts, incoherence, marked poverty of speech accompanied by a loss of emotional feeling.

Unipolar affective disorder (Depression)

Depression is also a recurrent disorder where an untreated episode usually lasts between 4–12 months (Kandal et al, 1991). Those who suffer from depression find it affects all aspects of their life: sleep is disturbed, appetite lost, thoughts are heavy, slow and gloomy, concentration becomes difficult and decisions impossible, actions slow down, and many are overwhelmed with feelings of worthlessness. Some are defeated by torpor and even the most mundane aspect of living, such as getting out of bed, appears momentous. A slowing down is not a characteristic symptom for all those with a unipolar affective disorder; some sufferers become agitated and restless. Finally, depression can deprive the suffering parent of the capacity to care about themselves or about those whom they love.

Life for the depressed appears hopeless and sufferers present a picture of misery and helpless worry.

Bipolar affective disorder (Manic-Depression)

About a quarter of people with major depression will also experience a manic episode. Although the depression is similar to that in the unipolar affective disorder, manic episodes are experienced as overwhelming surges of physical and mental energy. It is as if the floodgates have burst allowing a multitude of different thoughts and ideas to vie for expression. As a result sufferers become over-talkative, frequently to the point of incoherence. Others can become argumentative, dictatorial and haughty.

The feeling of physical energy results in restlessness and excitability, and the manic depressive feels driven to continual activity. When in this state sleep appears unnecessary, for some impossible, and eating an inconvenience that can be dispensed with.

Anxiety disorders

Although there are two main types of anxiety disorder, both are characterised by an irrational feeling of fear and impending doom. Sufferers experience a range of fear symptoms including: increased arousal, restlessness, sweating, heart palpitations, shortness of breath, trembling, and difficulties in concentration. They may experience chest pains and fear that they are dying or going crazy.

A 'panic attack' is one type of anxiety disorder. This is usually a brief, recurrent episode of terror which has no identifiable cause. Attacks commonly last 15–30 minutes although on rare occasions they may last for some hours. What distinguishes a panic attack from a legitimate fear response is its unexpectedness and occurrence in situations that do not normally evoke fear.

The other type of anxiety disorder is known as a 'generalised anxiety disorder'. In these cases sufferers experience unrealistic or excessive worries which are long lasting, 6 months is not unusual.

Personality disorder

Personality disorder implies abnormality in the sufferer's personal and interpersonal functioning. There are two major classificatory systems which offer definitions of personality disorder: ICD-10, World Health Organisation, 1992; and DSM-IV, American Psychiatric Association, 1994. The two systems, although not consistent with regard to the subcategories of personality disorder, do show some correspondence. However, the lack of consistency may be somewhat erroneous because it is generally accepted that many of those who suffer with a personality disorder demonstrate a number of different traits (Norton and Dolan, 1996).

The roots of adult personality disorders are thought to lie in early negative childhood experiences, including emotional, physical and sexual abuse (Herman et al, 1989; Westen et al, 1990). Personality disordered parents frequently have coexisting physical and mental health problems. Sufferers can experience long-term sequelae and react in a variety of ways including suicide attempts and self-mutilation. Alternatively, individuals may act out their stress through actual violence towards others (which can include partners or children), problem drinking or drug use, eating disorders, and sexual disinhibition.

The physical and psychological impact of drugs including alcohol

Alcohol, and to a lesser extent, drug use is well integrated into the lives of many parents. For example, drinking alcohol is an intrinsic element of most religious ceremonies, festive celebrations, meals, and everyday entertainment. Drinking or drug use can also be used to alter undesirable states such as depression, anxiety, withdrawals, symptoms of mental illness or the low self-esteem resulting from domestic violence. For the most part, people who use alcohol and drugs suffer few, if any, lasting adverse effects.

There are many types of drugs and each has an individual profile in terms of its main effects. However, the same drug may affect different people in different ways. The excessive consumption of alcohol will cause some people to simply fall asleep while others become aggressive and violent. The situation is further complicated because the same drug may have very different behavioural consequences even within the same individual depending on:

- current mental state
- experience and/or tolerance of the drug
- expectations
- personality
- means of administration (i.e. injecting, oral, smoking, nasal inhalation)
- dosage.

In examining the impact of different drugs it is important to bear in mind that most people do not consistently consume excessive amounts of alcohol or drugs. Occasional use of alcohol, or drugs such as cannabis and amphetamines, carries fewer risks of negative experiences. Intravenous drug use carries the additional risk of AIDS and hepatitis (van Beek et al, 1998).

Analgesics (include drugs such as heroin, morphine, methadone and distalgesics). The results of using these drugs is highly dependant upon the individual's level of tolerance, means of administration, and nature of the particular analgesic. Those who inject heroin experience an almost overwhelming pleasure (a 'rush') which lasts for a few seconds followed by a dreamlike, unreal state. People have described feeling relaxed, elated, calm and clear. Low dosage may have little effect on functioning, although at higher levels it produces sedation, sleepiness and unconsciousness (Coleman and Cassell, 1995).

Methadone (usually prescribed in an oral linctus form) induces a milder elation and no 'rush' because it is not ordinarily injected, though some users do grind up and inject methadone pills. Those who use the same daily dose may have minimal impairment of consciousness and many hold down responsible jobs and successfully raise families.

Withdrawals from heroin or other opiates like methadone can induce symptoms including nausea and vomiting, cramps, aches and pains, craving for the drug, sleeplessness, and lethargy. The experience has been likened to a severe case of the flu. If no new opiates are taken the symptoms will peak at some 72 hours after the last ingestion, although sleep problems, anxiety, and craving often continue.

Stimulants (amphetamines, cocaine, and 'crack' – a smokeable form of cocaine) produce feelings of elation, confidence, and happiness. Users become talkative and feel competent and powerful when under the influence of the drug. However, this is frequently a misperception as concentration is often impaired and in the cold light of non intoxication their efforts may not be as good as they thought. When used intravenously the impact is immediate, while oral or nasal intake results in a more delayed reaction. As the drug leaves their system users often experience feelings of hopelessness and depression.

The effect of amphetamines lasts for hours and for the most part, cocaine and 'crack' is more intensive but shorter acting. For some people excessive use of these drugs results in paranoia, hallucinations and other symptoms reminiscent of psychotic illness. For those suffering from mental illness stimulants may provoke a 'florid episode' leading to hospitalisation. Withdrawals can include depression, anxiety, craving, and sleep problems (Coleman and Cassell, 1995).

Depressants (alcohol, tranquillisers, sedatives and solvents) affect consciousness in different ways depending on the particular drug. Those who drink will, according to how much they drink, suffer from diminished capacity to concentrate, memory impairment, and reduced psychomotor co-ordination. Speech is often slurred and inhibitions lost, which can result in diminished self-control and violence (Coleman and Cassell, 1995). The effects of alcohol are mediated by tolerance, expectation, personality and social setting.

Tranquilliser users can feel calm and relaxed on small doses but consciousness may be lost when using larger doses or when mixed with alcohol. Such a cocktail is particularly dangerous because it enhances the consequences of alcohol while increasing the risk of overdose. The same is true of sedatives such as sleeping pills.

Withdrawals for alcohol range from the symptoms of a mild hangover to epileptic type fits, hallucinations, heavy perspiration, vomiting and tremulousness in the most severe cases. Tranquilliser and sedative withdrawals can include anxiety, irritability, sleeplessness and depression (Coleman and Cassell, 1995).

Hallucinogenic drugs (LSD, ecstasy, cannabis, 'magic mushrooms'). Cannabis is the mildest form of these drugs and is most commonly ingested through smoking. When smoked the effects begin about 10 or 15 minutes after the first inhalation. The user usually feels calm, relaxed, and has heightened awareness. Under the influence of cannabis memory is sometimes impaired, concentration becomes difficult and the user may lose all sense of time.

LSD and 'magic mushrooms' cause visual and other types of hallucinations which can last for 12 hours or more (especially with LSD and shorter periods for 'magic mushrooms'). Sensual experience will be enhanced or altered when under the influence of these drugs. Adverse reactions can be depersonalisation, hallucinations, paranoia and panic attacks but these are not common amongst those who use the drug moderately.

Withdrawals tend to include sleep problems, anxiety and sometimes mild cravings. 'Flashbacks' (a brief hallucinogenic experience – often less than a minute) can occur with LSD and less commonly with 'magic mushrooms', long after the initial experience.

For those with the most difficult and complex alcohol and drug problems, it is likely that problematic use will continue over time. Treatment may well prolong periods of abstinence or controlled use but relapse, in many cases, should be expected. The nature of most community services is such that many clients drop in and out of services according to their own needs, attitudes and behaviour. It should not be assumed that simply because a parent is receiving services that they are abstinent or even in control of their alcohol or drug use. Nor can it be assumed that if they have dropped out of treatment that they are problematically using alcohol or drugs.

The physical and psychological impact of domestic violence

The majority (80%) of reported incidents of domestic violence are assaults by men on women, a factor which suggests that men are more likely to be violent towards their partners than are women (Mayhew et al, 1993). However, epidemiological studies, which use the Conflict Tactics Scale (CTS) and involve self report questionnaires, question the role specificity of violence. Moffitt and Caspi's (1998) review of the research came to the conclusion that in partner violence women are equally likely to perpetrate the violence and that their assaults are not merely done in self-defence. They suggest that the reason behind domestic assaults is different for men and women. Generally women's assaults are motivated by fear and a desire to get 'equal', whereas men use violence and fear in order to control their partners.

But this position does not take account of the consequences of violence perpetrated by men compared to assaults by women. Men's superior strength generally means that women are at much greater risk of sustaining injuries in a domestic conflict. It is estimated that over 80% of reported assaults on women from partners involve injury and necessitate medical attention (Langley, 1991). In contrast women's assaults on male partners are rarely reported and there is little known about the incidence of injuries thus sustained. The emphasis on men's violence against women is also reflected by findings from the Duluth Community Abuse Programme in Minnesota (Pence and McMahon, 1998). Over an 18 year period, where female as well as male abusers were vigorously pursued within criminal justice strategies, women have never comprised more than 7% of those attending the perpetrators' programmes. An additional drawback to research findings based on the CTS, is that the scale fails to take account of the social context, severity of the assault or the controlling effect on the woman of threatened violence by their male partners (for example Dobash and Dobash, 1992; Ross, 1996).

Weighing the evidence from research, which suggests that on balance women are the main victims and survivors of domestic violence and, because little is known about the experiences of men (both as victims and perpetrators) in situations of domestic violence, this report concentrates on women's experiences. Moreover, in the majority of families, women assume the major share of children's care and when violence leads to family separation, children usually remain with the mother (Maidment, 1976; Eekelaar and Clive, 1977; Hardiker et al, 1991).

The impact of domestic violence on mothers can be extreme in that it can result in death either directly as a result of the assault (Home Office, 1994 statistics show that 43% of female murder victims are killed by partners or ex-partners) or indirectly through suicide (Mayhew et al, 1993). Domestic violence can also lead to injury severe enough to warrant medical attention, nearly a third of cases reported to the British Crime Survey required medical attention: 59% resulted in an injury and 13% in broken bones (British Crime Survey, 1996). Assault can take the form of slapping, punching, kicking, burns and stabbing, sexual abuse and rape, with the consequences being black eyes, bruising and broken bones (NCH, 1994; Kelly, 1994; Hester and Radford 1995).

Domestic violence is rarely confined to physical assaults but involves a mixture of physical and psychological violence.

> *'It was physical and mental. It was more mental violence…(but) it was physical as well. He's knocked me unconscious a few times and strangled me. He stabbed me once with a knife, but it was more mental, you know. He was driving me mad. I thought I was going crazy…'* (Malos and Hague, 1997, p.402).

Female victims can be exposed to emotional abuse, constant criticism, undermining and humiliation (Hester and Radford, 1995). Consequently, even when the impact is less obvious physically, domestic violence can have profoundly negative effects on women's mental health. There is considerable evidence that women exposed to domestic violence suffer a loss of confidence, depression, problems with sleep, increased isolation, and use medication and alcohol more frequently (see for example Mooney, 1994; Kelleher et al, 1995). Women who are victims of domestic violence feel degraded and see themselves merely as objects (Kirkwood, 1993). Indeed, Graham et al (1988) have likened the experiences of women living in violent relationships to that of hostages and victims of torture.

> *'I was a nervous wreck. I was just like a gibbering idiot. I had no confidence, no self esteem. I thought I was the most useless thing...because when you are being told all the time that you are crap, you sort of eventually begin to believe it'* (a mother quoted in NCH, 1994, p.45).

Domestic violence emerges over time, often after the relationship has become well established. The initial incident is rarely unambiguous and frequently the man initially begs forgiveness, offering reassurances and promises to change. In response many women blame themselves for the situation, turning their anger and sense of failure inward (Morely and Mullender, 1994; Kirkwood, 1993). Assaults, however, are rarely isolated incidents and after the initial attack, domestic violence can become a recurring theme. A recognised pattern frequently develops which may include: a build up of tension, eruption of violence, followed by pleas for forgiveness, a brief reunion and a return to former stability. Women's difficulties in leaving abusive men is reflected by the NCH report which shows the average duration of violent relationships to be 7.3 years (NCH, 1994).

Superficially, leaving a partner is an obvious solution for battered woman. Although some women do take this route out, the decision is rarely easy. Most women feel committed to their relationship, responsible for the children, some feel emotionally and financially dependant and believe they will be unable to survive on their own, and some feel that they or their children will be hurt or killed if they leave, or that their children will be taken into care (Pahl, 1985; Office of the Tanaiste, 1997). The decision to leave can place women and children in an increasingly vulnerable position. For many the point of departure triggers a violent assault by their male partner as he tries to exert control and prevent her departure (Kirkwood, 1993).

The fear that children will be removed is even more acutely felt when the abused woman is from an ethnic minority group. In these circumstances women may perceive official agencies as threatening, particularly if the woman is of refugee status, or believe their culture will be misinterpreted, or have little faith in their ability to explain their situation (Maitra, 1995; Hyton, 1997). This fear of statutory agencies is understandable, particularly when considering the over-representation of black children in the public care system (Courtney et al, 1996; Bernard quoted in McGee, 1996).

In spite of the difficulties of leaving home, it would be misleading to assume that all women submissively accept living in a violent relationship. Research has shown that some women do try to discuss the abuse with their partner, or talk to friends and relatives, while others call the police, or seek refuge (Browne and Saqi, 1987; Kelly, 1988; Hoff, 1990).

The impact on parenting

There are many ways which parental mental illness, excessive drinking or drug use or domestic violence can impact on parents' ability to look after their children. These include:

- parenting skills
- parents' perceptions
- control of emotions
- neglect of physical needs
- attachment
- separation.

Parenting skills

There is considerable research evidence which suggests mental illness, problem drinking or drug use, or domestic violence affects parenting skills. For example, apathy and listlessness, classic symptoms of depression, and which may be mirrored in those who use illicit drugs, mean parents have difficulty in organising their lives. As a result they are often unpredictable, inconsistent and ineffective with their children (see Davenport et al, 1984 for mental illness; Velleman, 1993 for problem drinking).

The impact on parenting may be indirect. Mothers who were not problem drug users but lived with a partner who was, were found to be psychologically distressed. Their distress was correlated (positively for girls and negatively for boys) with their children's depression (Greco-Vigorito et al, 1996).

Parents' perceptions

Domestic violence, parental mental illness, and problem alcohol and drug use can all affect parents' perceptions of the world. Excessive drinking or drug use, or the result of a violent attack can cause parents to lose consciousness. If the parent ensures that when this happens there is someone to look after the children then this matters little to the physical care of the child. However, when no provision has been made and no responsible adult is present, parental unconsciousness means children must fend for themselves. If children incur injury or fall ill during this time it is unlikely that many will be able to adequately attend to their own needs or know how or where to get help.

Mental illness, problem alcohol or drug use, or domestic violence can result in parents having a warped view of the world. Distorted parental perceptions can impact on parenting in a number of ways:

1. Research suggests that depressed mothers see themselves as inferior parents, less competent and adequate than non depressed parents (see for example Rutter, 1966; Weissman and Paykell, 1974; Davenport et al, 1984). Similar negative self perceptions have been found for women who are victims of domestic violence (see for example, Kelly, 1988; Kirkwood, 1993) and those with a drug problem (see Colton, 1980).

2. Depressed mothers see their children as having significantly more behavioural problems, a feature not substantiated by objective measures (Fergusson et al, 1995).

3. A mentally ill parent or those using hallucinogenic drugs or excess alcohol may have a distorted view of the child. For example, a particular child may be blamed for the parent's current distress, or alternatively, one child may be seen as a saviour and main source of solace (for mental illness see for example Rutter, 1990; for domestic violence see Emery, 1982).

Control of emotions

Depression can also make parents irritable and angry with children. In a study by Rutter and Quinton (1984) this was a prominent aspect of the behaviour of depressed parents towards children of school age. A personality disorder also influences the ability to control emotions. This is particularly evident during periods of stress such as when parents are having to deal with fractious infants or difficult adolescents (Norton and Dolan, 1996).

The intake of drugs such as cocaine crack or excessive amounts of alcohol can also produce violent mood swings from, for example, caring, loving and entertaining, to violent, argumentative and withdrawn. As a consequence parents with a drink or drug problem may behave in an inconsistent and frightening manner towards their children (see, for example, ChildLine, 1997). Users experiencing symptoms of 'withdrawal' may behave in unexpected ways which not only impact on children but have practice implications for the way social workers communicate with people in these circumstances.

Neglect of physical needs

The majority of children are not separated from mentally ill parents, or those who have problems with drink or drugs, or who are in unstable and violent relationships. The effects of domestic violence, problem drinking or drug use, or mental illness may mean that parents neglect their own and their children's physical needs. For example, although in situations of domestic violence most mothers reported that they had been able to continue to look after their children, for some mothers there were periods of despair when they didn't care what happened to either themselves or their children.

> *'At one time I went through a depression that went on for about a year where I didn't bother to do the housework, and I didn't bother to wash myself...I didn't give a shit about who said what about how the children looked...'* (NCH, 1994, p.47).

Attachment

In most cases parental problems influence how parents relate to their child. Weissman and Paykel (1974) observed that *'at the simplest level, the helplessness and hostility which are associated with acute depression interfere with the ability to be a warm and consistent mother'* (p.121). A psychopathic personality disorder may manifest itself in a *'callous unconcern for others, a low threshold for frustration, a discharge of aggression and an inability to feel remorse'* (Stroud, 1997, p.158). All these issues pose a considerable risk to the process of attachment. Similarly, drinking or drug use can result in the parent being emotionally unavailable to the child.

High levels of parental criticism are also associated with insecure attachments. Research suggests that children with opiate using parents are at increased risk because these mothers were observed to rely on harsh verbal responses when communicating with their children (Hogan, 1998).

It is possible that attachment between child and parent is insecure in families where a parent suffers mental illness, is a problem alcohol or drug user, or is in a violent relationship. As a result children may develop shaky internal working models which can have adverse consequences for later relationships (Howe, 1995). Moreover, children experience a degree of rejection which may have implications for the child's sense of connectedness. This in turn can affect intellectual, emotional, social and psychological functioning (Owusu-Bempah, 1995; Owusu-Bempah and Howitt, 1997).

A further problem noted by Rutter (1989) is that depressed mothers have a tendency to seek comfort from a daughter. Although in some cases this can result in a warm and mutually satisfying relationship, in other instances the child may be used inappropriately for comfort (Radke-Yarrow et al, 1988). In addition, children may take on too much responsibility for their age, or be drawn into a behavioural style of distress and depression (Rutter 1990; Amato, 1991).

Summarising the effects of depression on mothers, major depression can cause mothers:

- to be insensitive to their children's needs
- to be unresponsive to their cues
- to express more anger and
- to be more critical of their children.

(Weissman et al, 1972; Pound et al, 1984; Radke-Yarrow et al, 1985; Radke-Yarrow et al, 1988; Cummings and Davies, 1994). Much research has shown that these traits are amongst the strongest and most reliable predictors of insecure parent-child attachment (see Bowlby, 1969; Ainsworth et al, 1978; Egeland and Scroufe, 1981). It is hardly surprising then to find considerable evidence to suggest maternal depression is associated with insecure maternal-child attachments (Radke-Yarrow et al, 1985; Spieker and Booth, 1988).

Separation

When parents' problems become extreme they may result in children being separated from one or both parents. For example, drug dealing to sustain a 'habit' may lead to the parent's imprisonment, domestic violence to a mother's escape to a refuge, or an acute episode of mental illness to hospitalisation. When this happens the care of the children may fall to others. If the other parent or close relative can provide a stable environment and the time and attention the children require, the risk of negative effects of uncontrolled emotions is much reduced. The luxury of a second caring relative is not always available. For these children the hospitalisation or imprisonment of one parent results in the child being 'looked after' by the local authority, with all the well known concomitant difficulties surrounding placement.

The social consequences

Parental mental illness, problematic alcohol and drug use, or domestic violence are associated with a variety of social consequences which are similar to those for families receiving child care social work support (Brown and Harris, 1978; Sheppard, 1993 and 1997).

Although these are explored from the starting point of parental problems, it is important to note that mental illness, problem drinking, or drug use may be understandable reactions to intolerable life circumstances (Brown and Harris, 1978). Indeed, some feminist analysis suggests that women's depression or problem drinking should be seen as a psychological indicator of their oppression (Corob, 1987; Velleman, 1993).

Three issues are of particular significance for parenting: the impact on living standards; the loss of friends and family; and the disruption of family relationships.

Impact on living standards

Uncontrolled and unpredictable behaviour can have financial consequences. For example, the bizarre behaviour of the schizophrenic, the weariness and inactivity of the depressive, or the fear and terror of the anxious, can make it difficult to sustain a job. Similarly, the uncontrolled and exaggerated mood swings and irritability associated with problem drinking and drug misuse can affect the parent's ability to keep a job. Some 50% of people treated for problem drinking have been sacked because of their problem (Velleman, 1993).

When jobs are lost family income is reduced. Canadian research suggests unemployment is high among parents using cocaine crack – only 7% of families had salaries as the main source of income (Leslie, 1993). Moreover, the parent's customary ways of managing money may be hampered because delusions or irrational fears have resulted in strange spending patterns.

Living standards can also be adversely affected because family income is used to sustain parents' alcohol or drug use. Coleman and Cassell (1995) estimate that a 'reasonable income' can support alcohol or methadone habits but only the very rich can afford to fund the continued use of heroin or cocaine. To sustain excessive drinking and drug use, for many parents, an alternative source of income must be found. To get the necessary money parents may allow the home to be used for criminal activities such as drug dealing or prostitution (Hogan, 1998). The home may also be jeopardised because money for rent and essential household bills, such as for food, heating, and clothing, is used to satisfy parental needs, or bills are simply overlooked or regarded as irrelevant (Velleman, 1996).

The impact of criminal activities, which may result from seeking extra income, may place children at risk of significant harm in several ways (Swadi, 1994). Exposure to criminal behaviour may affect children's attitudes to authority and crime (Hogan, 1998). Prostitution may result in even very young children observing or being drawn into inappropriate sexual activity (Cleaver and Freeman, 1996).

Violent and aggressive outbursts are associated with domestic violence, problem drinking or drug use and the life style associated with drug dealing. Such incidents can result in adults deliberately damaging and destroying property. When this takes place within the home the fabric of the house may be destroyed and the place becomes unsafe for children to live in.

Apart from children being exposed to dangers, parental problems may also result in neglect of the children. Homes need to offer warmth, sanitation and shelter and to reach basic standards of hygiene. The effects of mental illness, problem drinking and drug use, or domestic violence on parents' consciousness and energy, can result in the living space being littered with food scraps, or heavily polluted with human or animal faeces. Such circumstances can pose serious risks to children's health (Thoburn et al, in preparation). Excessive alcohol or illicit drug use may also mean drugs and used needles and syringes are easily accessible to the child and a lack of supervision may result in experimentation.

However, this is not always the scenario, because some families where alcohol and illicit drug use is a problem continue to ensure the children are clean and fed (Brisby et al, 1997). They make adequate provision for their children and thus ensure that they are not exposed to environmental dangers. For example, parental forethought can ensure adequate substitute child care arrangements so that children are not privy to drinking binges or drug misuse. Careful attention to storage means that unsafe substances or equipment are not accessible to children. In addition, a caring partner or relative of a mentally ill parent can make sure that essential household services are intact, that the home is sanitary and safe for the child.

Finally, there are financial implications for children when parental difficulties result in separation and divorce. It is widely acknowledged that separation and divorce have financial costs for both parties, with women generally at a disadvantage in the job and housing market (Hague and Malos, 1994). But when families break up because of domestic violence this is exacerbated because overwhelmingly it is women and children who have to leave their home. Many will need somewhere safe and secret to go to in the short term and later more permanent accommodation. The imposed move and the increased child care responsibilities often bring with them job losses for mothers and increased problems for securing alternative work. It is hardly surprising, therefore, to learn that a major reason many women remain with violent men is their lack of economic resources and having nowhere to go (Hague and Malos, 1994; Office of the Tanaiste, 1997).

Loss of friends and family

The increasing withdrawal from reality or obsession with self, whether due to mental illness, or problem alcohol or drug use, affects relationships with family and friends. Self-absorption bores even the most faithful, and bizarre behaviour and incoherent conversation, or violent outbursts generate unease and fear (Kandal et al, 1991).

Friendships may also be curtailed because mothers in violent relationships wish to hide their experience. *'I was ashamed', 'I was too embarrassed', 'No one would have believed me', 'I had no friends left I could tell'*, were all reasons given by women for keeping their abuse secret (NCH, 1994, p.79). The NCH (1994) survey of mothers attending family centres found few had told anyone about the violence when it first happened. Women subjected to domestic violence may also keep silent about their experiences through fear and a lack of opportunity to develop close and confiding relationships.

> *'I was kept in one room for six years. Six years of my life was in one room and kitchen. He kept me there. He wouldn't let me go out except sometimes with him...And if anything he didn't like about the cooking and the shopping, he'd start doing the beating. Just like I was his slave...'* (Asian woman who had three children in Malos and Hague, 1997, p.403).

Parents may cut themselves off from family and friends because they are ashamed or frightened, or because they have stolen from them, or do not wish to see their abusive partner's family. As a result, these families can become isolated and lack the support needed to ensure their children are safely parented.

When parents are drug users research suggests that they often base their social activities around the procurement and use of the drug. For example, Canadian research on families where at least one parent uses cocaine crack, found that in over a quarter (28%) of cases the family lived with others who also used crack. Children living in these circumstances have been found to be at increased risk of physical and sexual abuse (see for example, Johnston, 1990 quoted in Leslie, 1993) and a lack of supervision, exposure to strangers and violence (Leslie, 1993).

A further critical factor is the likelihood that drug abusing families will experience greater levels of community rejection and be less involved in religious, neighbourhood or cultural activities. Women appear to be particularly affected. Problem drug using women reported higher levels of loneliness and social isolation than men in similar circumstances (Hogan, 1998).

Disruption of family relationships

Much research has shown the negative impact on children of divorce, marital disharmony and domestic violence. Indeed, there is a considerable body of evidence to suggest that parental mental illness, or problem drinking or drug use, which is not accompanied by other family stressors, presents fewer risks to the children (for mental illness see Quinton and Rutter, 1985; for problem drinking see Velleman, 1993). The impact is also likely to be ameliorated when family life is harmonious and one parent is available to ensure the emotional and physical well being of the children (for mental illness see Quinton and Rutter, 1985; Feldman et al, 1987; in terms of problem drinking, see Casswell, 1991; Velleman, 1993; Brisby et al, 1997).

However, in spite of the possibility of positive outcome in some cases, mental illness or problem alcohol or drug use can place considerable strain on relationships between spouses or intimate partners. Problem drinking and drug use is associated with domestic violence (Coleman and Cassell, 1995). More than 30% of problem drinkers receiving treatment believed marital conflict was a result of their drinking. Furthermore it has been estimated that 80% of cases of domestic violence are alcohol related (Velleman, 1993).

There is also considerable evidence that mental illness is associated with marital breakdown because coping on a day to day basis with a depressed partner can be very exhausting and dispiriting (Weissman and Paykel, 1974). Moreover, the risk to marital breakdown is further increased when a depressed person marries someone with a psychiatric illness; a situation which is not uncommon (Merikangas and Spiker, 1982). When this happens the symptoms of depression become more severe, and marital and family disruption more likely (Merikangas et al, 1998). The link between mental illness and marital discord is highest when parents suffer from personality disorder.

The association between mental illness or problem drinking and domestic violence is complex (Rutter and Quinton, 1984; Kelly, 1994). For example, not only may the psychiatric disorder or problem drinking or drug use result in marital discord, but women may develop mental health problems, or turn to drugs and alcohol as a direct consequence of domestic violence (Velleman, 1993; Farmer and Owen, 1995). Alternatively, domestic violence and mental illness, problem alcohol or drug use, may be related to a prior condition (such as childhood adversities).

To sum up

The psychological impact

- Children do not necessarily experience behavioural or emotional problems when parents suffer mental illness, problem drinking or drug use, or domestic violence. However, when these parental problems coexist the risk to children increases considerably.

- Mental illness can seriously effect functioning. The impact of schizophrenia, depression, anxiety disorders, and personality disorder are individually explored. For example, the delusions and hallucinations suffered by the schizophrenic are shown to result in a preoccupation with a private world. Depression can result in children being neglected because feelings of gloom, worthlessness and hopelessness mean everyday activities are left undone. Regardless of its cause, mental illness can blunt parents' emotions and feelings, or cause them to behave towards their children in bizarre or violent ways.

- The effects of alcohol and drugs varies according to: the type of drug, the amounts taken and means of administration, the individual's physical make-up, experience and/or tolerance of the drug, the user's personality and current mental state. The consequences of taking alcohol and a range of illicit drugs have been explored.

- In situations of domestic violence women are the main victims and survivors. Domestic violence involves both physical assaults and psychological abuse. Both can have a negative impact on women's ability to look after their children. Many women have difficulty in ending the violence because they fear leaving a violent partner or asking help from outsiders. For example, a partner may have threatened their own lives and those of their children. Some women believe they will not survive emotionally or financially without their partner. Furthermore, many women fear their children will be taken into care if their situation becomes public knowledge.

The impact on parenting

- Parental problems can result in parents having difficulty organising their lives. This may result in inconsistent and ineffective parenting.

- When parents lose consciousness or contact with reality, children's physical safety and emotional well being may be at risk.

- Parental problems may mean parents have difficulty controlling their emotions. Violent, irrational or withdrawn behaviour can frighten children.

- When parents' experience feelings of depression or despair, or when drink or drugs divorce them from reality, they may neglect their own and their children's physical needs.

- Children may be insecurely attached because mental illness, problem drinking or drug use, or domestic violence has meant parents are insensitive, unresponsive, angry and critical of their children.

- When parents' behaviour becomes extreme children may have to be cared for by someone else. If the other parent or relative can respond to the child's needs negative effects are minimised.

The social consequences

- These three parental problems can impact on the family's standard of living because:

(a) Family income may drop. Bizarre or unpredictable behaviour makes jobs difficult to sustain.

(b) Family income may be used satisfy parental needs. Purchasing food and clothing or paying essential household bills may be sacrificed.

(c) To sustain parental habits, alternative sources of income may draw families into criminal activities.

(d) Parents' behaviour can result in basic standards of hygiene being neglected.

(e) Separation, particularly as the result of domestic violence, can result in mothers and children having to move, with all the concomitant problems.

- Families can become isolated because relationships with family and friends are affected. This can have a number of causes: bizarre or unpredictable behaviour can alienate friends and family; families wish to hide their experiences; friends and social activities are based around parents' current needs and circumstances.

- Relationships within families can be disrupted. Mental illness and problem drinking and drug use is associated with marital breakdown. The association is complex. Mental illness or problem drinking or drug use may strain relationships, or they may be a consequence of an unhappy or violent relationship. Alternatively, all may have a common cause, such as childhood adversity.

Part three:

Which children are most at risk of suffering significant harm?

Vulnerable children

The seriousness of the parental problem, be it mental illness, alcohol or drug use, or domestic violence is less relevant than the level to which the child is directly involved. Most at risk of suffering significant harm are children who become the victims of aggressive acts or hostile behaviour, or are neglected for pathological reasons, or suffer from parental rejection (Quinton and Rutter, 1985).

This risk increases when children become targets of their parents' delusions (Stroud, 1997). For example, the child of mentally ill parents may be forced to participate in parental rituals and compulsions, or parental illness can result in marked restrictions in the child's social activities (Rutter, 1966). In domestic disputes children can be abused or even murdered as acts of revenge or retaliation aimed at punishing the warring partner (Wilcynski quoted in Toolis,1998).

However, research also suggests that simply witnessing parental distress can have adverse effects on children. The NCH (1994) study on domestic violence found that children spoke about their distress at seeing their mother's physical and emotional suffering. *'He would come in and rip my mother's clothes off. He tried to strangle her, just beat her up like...We were always watching it...'* (child quoted in the NCH, 1994, p.31). Although parents generally try to shield their children from witnessing incidents of domestic violence, some fathers insist that children watch the abuse of their mother (Hester and Radford, 1995). As a high proportion (90% noted in a study by Hamner, 1989) of incidents of domestic violence are witnessed by children, the impact may be considerable.

To protect their mothers, children may try to intervene. Hamner (1989) found children often called out the police or urged their mother to separate. But separation did not always bring an end to children's problems because many found themselves in the role of peace keeper.

> *'The mothers said that the children often tried to minimise the harm or keep the peace by holding back information from father to mother, mediating between the two and covering up or toning down the violence and threats of abuse'.*

Joseph Rowntree Foundation (1996).

The violence itself did not necessarily stop on separation. Hester and Radford (1996) found the majority of mothers were attacked or threatened or verbally abused when taking or collecting children from contact visits. Separation therefore did not necessarily put an end to children having to see their mother being abused. In addition, Hester and Radford (1996) note that there were many incidents of child abuse and neglect reported as a result of contact visits.

Although there is considerable evidence to suggest that children can be protected from the adverse effects of parental mental illness and problem drug and alcohol use, as discussed below, there is little or no evidence for this in the case of domestic violence. Indeed, it is the association with domestic violence that is most frequently cited as presenting the greatest risk of suffering significant harm to children when parents suffer mental illness, or are problem drinkers or drug users.

What can be identified are factors which aggravate the impact of domestic violence:

- the combination with problem drinking or drug misuse
- witnessing the parent's sexual and physical abuse
- being drawn into participating in the abuse of a parent
- colluding in the secrecy and concealment of the assaults (Hamner, 1989; Jaffe, Wolfe and Wilson, 1990).

Protective factors

No one age group of childhood seems either particularly protected from or damaged by the impact of parental mental illness (see, for example, d'Orban, 1979), alcohol or drug problems (see, for example, Rivinus, 1991; Velleman, 1996). Individual variations in how children respond are in part a function of the severity, characteristics, and social context of their parents' problems. Research suggests children are less likely to be affected adversely from parental mental illness when it is:

- mild
- of short duration
- unassociated with family discord, conflict and disorganisation
- unassociated with the family breaking up
- linked with children having good social networks, especially with adults

(Post, 1962; Rutter, 1990).

These factors are equally relevant when parents have drink or drug problems. There are, however, a number of additional ones which have been identified as key:

- one parent has no problems with alcohol or drug use
- parent(s) in treatment
- other responsible adults are involved in child care
- maintenance of family rituals and activities
- drugs, needles, syringes are out of reach of children
- stable home, adequate financial resources.

(Herjanic et al, 1979; Blane, 1988; Casswell, 1991; Velleman, 1993; Hill et al, 1996).

Children's ability to cope with parental adversity is also related to their age, gender and individual personality. With regard to gender there is some evidence to suggest that children of the same sex as a mentally ill parent are at greater risk of developing the disorder. This is particularly so with the development of depression in girls (Goodyer et al, 1993). A more widely applicable phenomenon is the finding that girls are less affected in the short term, but as parental problems continue they are just as likely to exhibit distress as boys (for domestic violence see Hetherington et al, 1978, with relation to problem alcohol and drug use see Werner, 1986; Tweed, 1991, for parental mental illness see Rutter, 1985; Stewart et al, 1980).

Rutter (1985) suggests that a child's ability to cope with adversity is not the result of a specific factor or coping mechanism. What is of importance is that children have developed the necessary strengths which will enable them to find ways to cope with different situations. He notes that this is related to children having:

- A sense of self-esteem and self-confidence
- A belief in one's self-efficacy and ability to deal with change and adaptation
- A repertoire of social problem solving approaches.

Protective factors which are likely to foster such a cognitive set include a secure, stable, affectionate relationship and experiences of success and achievement (Rutter, 1985).

It is important that professionals do not pathologise all children who live in families where a parent suffers from mental illness, has problems with alcohol and drugs, or is in a violent relationship. As we have already noted, although these issues serve to qualify children as 'in need' (Department of Health, 1997a) a significant proportion show no long-term behavioural or emotional disturbance. Nonetheless, the health and development of a considerable number of children living in these circumstances are adversely affected and would benefit from services.

Although some findings are general to children of any age it is important to highlight how these parental problems impact on children on various developmental dimensions at different ages, in order to understand what services might be needed to ensure their needs are met.

To sum up

Factors which increase vulnerability

- The children most at risk of suffering significant harm are those involved in parental delusions, and children who become targets for parental aggression or rejection, or are neglected for pathological reasons.

- To witness parental distress and suffering can have an adverse psychological impact on children.

- The negative impact of domestic violence is exacerbated when: the violence is combined with drink or drug use; children witness the abuse; are drawn into the abuse; or collude in concealing the assaults.

Protective factors

- The adverse effects on children are less likely when parental problems are: mild; of short duration; unassociated with family discord and disorganisation; and do not result in the family breaking up.

- Children may also be protected when the other parent or a family member can respond to the child's developmental needs. In relation to problem drinking or drug use, children's safety also depends on drugs and alcohol, needles and syringes not being easily available.

- Children's ability to cope is related to their age, gender and individual personality. Children of the same gender as the parent experiencing problems may be at greater risk. Boys tend to be more at risk than girls in the short term, but when problems endure girls are similarly affected.

- Children's ability to cope is related to: a sense of self-esteem and self-confidence; feeling in control and capable of dealing with change; and having a range of approaches for solving problems. Such traits are fostered by secure, stable and affectionate relationships and experiences of success and achievement.

- A significant proportion of children show no long-term behavioural or emotional disorders when exposed to parental mental illness, problem drinking or drug use, or domestic violence. However, a considerable number of children do exhibit symptoms of disturbance and would benefit from services.

Part four:

Child development and parenting capacity

Although there are, in general, factors which place children more or less vulnerable to the behaviours which result from their parents' problems, the impact on children will vary depending on their age and stage of development. Therefore, it seems appropriate to look in more detail at the different stages of development. This review has been deliberately confined to the findings from research which may mean that factors which are more readily identified from clinical and professional practice have been omitted. These are no less important as a source of evidence but are beyond the scope of this report.

In exploring the research findings six stages of childhood are discussed:

- The unborn child
- Children aged 0–2 years
- Children aged 3–4 years
- Children aged 5–9 years
- Children aged 10–14 years
- Children 15 years and older.

To provide a context for the problems which can result for children each section is prefaced with a discussion of expected development.

The unborn child

Clearly it is not relevant in relation to the unborn child, to explore the range of developmental dimensions which are looked at for children once they are born. Instead, the focus is on the ways parental mental illness, problem drinking or drug use, or domestic violence affect the unborn child both through genetic transmission and environmental impact.

Although there is considerable information concerning the effects on the unborn child of maternal alcohol and drug consumption, what is known about the impact of maternal mental illness or domestic violence is more limited.

Conditions needed for optimal development of the unborn child

The unborn child needs nourishment and a safe environment in order to develop. Regular visits to the ante-natal clinic can help ensure that the health of both the expectant mother and the developing child are monitored. To address the nutritional needs of the unborn baby the expectant mother requires an adequate diet. A safe environment means that expectant mothers should avoid contact with viruses such as Rubella and avoid unnecessary medication. The devastating effects on children of women who took thalidomide are still evident. In addition, there is increasing evidence that expectant mothers should not smoke tobacco excessively. Babies born to heavy smokers are likely to suffer a higher risk of spontaneous abortion, still-births and the possibility of low birth weight with its consequent negative effects (Julien, 1995).

The environment in which the mother lives and works also has an impact on the growing foetus. Physical impacts, collisions, bumps or blows which may jar or dislodge the foetus need to be avoided. In addition, where the expectant mother lives may also have an adverse effect on the developing foetus. For example, highly polluted cities, the routine discharge of dangerous chemicals or nuclear leaks may have adverse effects on the unborn child.

Finally, there is growing evidence to suggest that the mother's emotional condition has an effect on the unborn child. Recent research suggests that maternal stress can release hormones which pass through the placenta. Simultaneously, severe stress can increase the mother's blood pressure and by implication decrease uterine blood flow. The overall result can be lower birth weight (Wolkind, 1981; Reading, 1983). Not all studies have consistently shown stress to be related to low birth weight. Anxiety in women with no previous or current mental health problems was not found to correlate with low birth weight (Burstein et al, 1974).

The effect of mental illness on the unborn child

The issues affecting the unborn child relate to both genetics and environment. Rutter (1989), in his comprehensive review of studies on parental mental illness as a psychiatric risk factor for children, notes that much of the research is based on the premise that genetics play a significant role. Genetic transmission is shown to be a factor in cases of schizophrenia and major affective disorders (see Fombonne, 1995 for data on depressive disorders) and anti-social personality disorders. Rutter argues that the best evidence for the genetic hypothesis comes from rates of disorder in children of mentally ill parents who are adopted in infancy and brought up by carers who do not suffer from a mental illness. Evidence for a heredity link was shown in cases of schizophrenia (Rutter, 1989). However, in more commonly occurring types of mental illness such as depression, heredity appears to be a less important factor (Torgersen, 1983).

A study by Wolkind (1981) found babies born to mothers suffering a psychiatric illness during pregnancy were of lower birth weight than babies born to mothers without a psychiatric illness during pregnancy. However, a direct causal link was difficult to establish because significantly more mothers in the psychiatric group smoked and attendance at ante-natal clinic was worse than for well mothers.

The effect of drugs including alcohol on the unborn child

There is little dispute that excessive parental drinking or drug use negatively affects the unborn child (Rosett, 1980; Plant, 1985; National Institute on Alcohol Abuse and Alcoholism, 1990; Avis, 1993; Juliana and Goodman, 1997). What is in dispute is the degree and nature of that impact.

The effect of drinking or drugs on the developing foetus is dependent on three inter-related factors: the pharmacological make-up of the drug, the gestation of pregnancy, and the route/amount/duration of drug use (Rosett, 1980; Julien, 1995; Gerada, 1996). The foetus is most susceptible to structural damage during 4–12 weeks of gestation; drugs taken later generally affect growth or cause neo-natal addiction (Julien, 1995).

The effects of cocaine and heroin are particularly damaging because they may cause placental detachment, still birth, premature birth, low birth weight and microcephaly. Babies may also be born addicted (Julien, 1995; Gerada, 1996). The effects on the unborn child of newer drugs such as ecstasy are not well researched.

The transmission of HIV infection across the placenta to the unborn child is a serious complication of intravenous drug use. Research suggests 13–37% of babies born to infected mothers (in developed countries) are infected (European Collaborative Study, 1991). The unborn child is also at risk of contracting hepatitis C virus if the expectant mother injects drugs. Research suggests that the unborn child is vulnerable even when the expectant mother is HIV negative (Resti et al, 1998).

In relation to alcohol there is a consensus that excessive use of alcohol during pregnancy by the mother can cause foetal alcohol syndrome which may damage the central nervous system and result in a range of anatomical abnormalities and behaviour problems (Plant, 1985; Abel, 1997).

Adverse effects on the unborn child are not confined to maternal drinking. There is some evidence to suggest that fathers who are heavy drinkers produce children with lower birth weight and increased risk of heart defects (Plant, 1997). Furthermore, spontaneous abortion and neo-natal deaths are associated with excessive drinking of either parent (Royal College of Physicians, 1995).

Research conducted in the USA identifies a less severe manifestation of foetal alcohol syndrome, labelled foetal alcohol effect. Symptoms include poor feeding, tremors, irritability, occasional seizures and increased risk of sudden death syndrome (Avis, 1993; Julien, 1995). Finally, there is some evidence from North America that there may be a link between any alcohol use in pregnancy and spontaneous abortion, but this evidence is refuted by European and Australian research (Abel and Sokol, 1991).

Two further complicating factors in gauging the impact of maternal drug use on the unborn child, are the combination of substances taken and the pattern of alcohol or drug use. For example, women who use heroin regularly are also likely to use tobacco, cannabis, stimulants and tranquillisers. Moreover, the quantity and pattern of alcohol or drug use can vary from day to day (Plant, 1985).

There is considerable evidence to suggest that the more frequent the use and the larger the quantities of alcohol or drugs ingested, the greater the impact on the unborn child (Cork, 1969; Rivinus, 1991; Julien, 1995). Even this agreed evidence must be tempered by further factors which suggest how complex it may be to predict outcomes for individuals. For example, moderate, regular alcohol or drug intake during pregnancy may be less harmful than 'binge' use, which can place the foetus at risk from sudden withdrawal (Plant, 1997).

All the problems associated with problem alcohol and drugs use could be ameliorated to some extent by good ante-natal care. However, many pregnant drug users do not come for ante-natal care until late in pregnancy because opiates, such as heroin, often affect menstruation and women are uncertain of dates (Dawe, et al, 1992; Julien, 1995). Others may fear that revealing their drug use to antenatal care staff will result in the involvement of social services and the possible loss of the baby once it is born (Dore and Dore, 1995; Burns, 1996).

Finally, while there is general agreement that alcohol and drug use can increase risk, it is also probable that most mothers who use alcohol or drugs will give birth to healthy, normal children who suffer from no long term effects (Werner, 1986).

The effect of domestic violence on the unborn child

In this section the impact on the unborn child of domestic violence is reviewed. There are three main possible ways: inherited traits, physical damage to the foetus, and the effects of maternal stress.

Unlike mental illness, there is no direct evidence to show genetics plays a role in the transmission of domestic violence. However, it might be argued that the evidence of an association between parental personality disorder and conduct disturbance in boys stems from a single source (Rutter and Quinton, 1984).

The foetus may be damaged because the state of pregnancy can increase both the severity and frequency of abuse for women living in a violent relationship. Domestic violence threatens the unborn children because domestic assaults on pregnant women frequently include punches or kicks directed at the abdomen. Research on domestic violence from both America (McFarlane quoted in Morley and Mullender, 1994) and Northern Ireland (McWilliams and McKiernan, 1993) suggests this was the experience of between 40–60% of battered women during pregnancy. The assaults result in an increased chance of miscarriage, stillbirth, premature birth, foetal brain injury and fractures, placental separation, rupture of the mother's spleen, liver or uterus (Casey, 1987; Andrews and Brown, 1988).

Studies of the effects on the unborn child of mother's stress suggest marital disharmony is associated with increased childhood morbidity such as physical illness, developmental lag, neurological dysfunction and behavioural disturbance (Stott, 1973). The association may be indirect because domestic violence may lead mothers to become so depressed that they fail to look after their physical needs during pregnancy. *'I just didn't care. He was so cruel that I didn't take any pride in myself...I lost the baby...I was only seven stone'* (NCH,1994, p.47). Finally, domestic violence may place the unborn child at risk because women tend to be late or poor attendees for ante-natal care (Hester and Radford, 1995).

To sum up

Key problems for the unborn child
- Genetic transmission of some forms of mental illness.

- Foetal damage brought about by intake of harmful substances. The impact will depend on which substances are taken, the stage of the pregnancy when drugs are ingested, and the route, amount and duration of drug use.

- Foetal damage as a result of physical violence. This may include foetal fracture, brain injury and organ damage.

- Spontaneous abortion, premature birth and low birth weight, and still birth.

Protective factors
- Good regular ante-natal care.

- Adequate nutrition, income support and housing for the expectant mother.

- The avoidance of viruses, unnecessary medication, smoking and severe stress.

- Support for the expectant mother of at least one caring adult.

- An alternative, safe and supportive residence for expectant mothers subject to violence and the threat of violence.

The impact on children

A review of the evidence on the impact of parental mental health, problem alcohol and drug use, or domestic violence suggests that the effects on children's development may have many features in common, irrespective of the source of the problem. Accordingly, the following sections attempt to draw together factors where the outcome is similar. However, it remains necessary to highlight specific outcomes which are associated with a discrete problem.

Children aged 0–2 years

Health

Expected health
During the first few weeks of life babies are expected to achieve a balanced state with regard to feeding, sleeping and elimination. Parents or carers need to take babies regularly to clinics for immunisations and developmental reviews.

Babies' development follows a recognised pattern and they generally achieve their milestones within the anticipated time frame. Babies with health problems, or with learning or physical disabilities, for example, sight or hearing problems, should receive appropriate and prompt professional attention.

The home should be suitable for the baby and offer adequate safety and protection. Babies and infants who are ill or injured should get the attention they need, and periodic bouts of illness should generally have a recognised medical source.

The possible impact of parental problem

There are three main ways that an infant's health may be damaged: foetal damage, parents behaviour, and poor physical environment.

The effects of heroin or other opiates on the foetus can cause new born babies to show any number of the following withdrawal symptoms: irritating and high pitched crying, rapid breathing and heart rate, disturbed sleep pattern, sweating and fever, vomiting and diarrhoea and feeding difficulties (see Hogan 1998). At its most extreme, withdrawal of the drugs can result in the death of the new born child through generalised seizures (Gerada, 1996). A more common result is that babies born to drug addicted mothers are underweight, although weight gain has been reported in many cases, especially when good health and social care is given. When mothers are infected with HIV their newly born babies are at risk because the virus can be transmitted via breast milk and maternal secretions (see Johnson and Johnson, 1993 for more detailed information).

Babies and infants may also be harmed because of parents' behaviour. Children under five were found to account for 81% of children killed or severely injured by parents. No statistical difference was found with regard to the average age of child victims when the parent's psychiatric health was taken into account (Falkov, 1996). This finding is in line with Rutter's (1966) work which showed infants were most at risk from parental mental illness, when they were the victims of aggressive acts or hostile behaviour, or were neglected or suffered parental rejection.

Infants may also be harmed when parents' concentration is impaired because of mental illness, excessive alcohol intake or drug misuse. When this happens mothers may be less attentive to the baby's health needs (see Rutter, 1989 for the data on impact of mental illness). For example, the mother may not be able to concentrate long enough to complete breast feeding or nappy changing. Similarly, she may pose a risk to the baby's general safety, for example, when bathing the infant, or in ensuring the environment is safe for a toddler (Cassin, 1996). Furthermore, the disabling effects of mental illness, problem drinking or drug use, or domestic violence may result in routine health checks being missed, or inadequate intervention being sought when the infant is unwell.

Perhaps most worrying is when infants are used as accessories in the abuse of their mother. Hester and Radford (1995) record a particularly horrifying case where *'the infant child had been wrapped in a sheet by the father and used as a weapon with which to batter the mother'* (Hester and Radford, 1995, p.52).

Finally, it is important to remember the effects of social deprivation. There is a well established association between poor material conditions and illness in small children (see Bradshaw, 1990). The poor material conditions may not necessarily be the result of parental problems, but may have contributed significantly to parental stress (Brown and Harris, 1978).

Education and cognitive ability

Expected ability

Soon after birth babies respond to sound and voices. During the first year they learn to babble, put sounds together and understand requests such as 'give it to me'. By two years there is a marked increase in vocabulary and simple directions are able to be followed.

During the first two years of life babies gain control over their bodies. At 3–4 months most can roll over and grasp objects. Sitting up is achieved at around 6–9 months and standing and walking generally between 12–24 months.

At around 6 months many babies engage in social play such as 'peek-a-boo'. There is an increasing interest in play and simple stories are enjoyed (Fahlberg, 1991; Smith and Cowie, 1991).

Pretend or fantasy play starts at approximately 12–15 months. Early pretend play depends heavily on realistic objects such as cups and combs etc. As infants get older substitute objects can be used, for example, a wooden block for a 'cake', or a stick for a 'sword' (Smith and Cowie, 1991).

The possible impact of parental problems

The main impact of parental problems on babies results from inconsistent or neglectful behaviour. Environmental factors are also important.

In relation to mental illness, the impact on cognitive development tends to result from parents' behaviour. When the mother suffers from depression the baby's cognitive development may be affected because there is less interaction between mother and baby. Depressed mothers, or those with alcohol or drug problems, have been shown to respond less frequently to their baby's cues and when they did respond, are more likely to do so in a controlling rather than facilitative manner (see Cox et al, 1987 for mental health; and Hill et al, 1996; Juliana and Goodman, 1997 for alcohol and drugs). Depressed mothers are also less likely to modify their behaviour according to the behaviour of their infant (Bettes, 1988).

The evidence on how this may impact on children's cognitive development is not clear. On the one hand, some research suggests maternal depression is associated with negative consequences for infants. Expressive language is delayed (Cox et al, 1987) and the child's ability to concentrate and complete simple tasks is worse than for children of well mothers (Breznitz and Friedman, 1988).

On the other hand, an observational study of 2–3 year old infants of depressed and non-depressed mothers found no overall differences in terms of the child's temperament, language or mental state (Pound et al, 1988). So the case remains unproved.

It may be that the behaviour of parents is less important than the psycho/social environment in which children are growing up. Rutter (1989) suggests the differences in research findings are due to other associative factors, such as poverty, marital conflict and paternal psychiatric history, factors which these studies do not take into account.

Identity and social presentation

Expected identity and social presentation
Infants after the age of 12 months start to develop an independent sense of self. At two years they are relatively confident in themselves and their abilities. They expect to be liked by adults and see adults as dependable and trustworthy (Smith and Cowie, 1991). Most mothers take pride in ensuring that their baby is clean and dressed appropriately.

The possible impact of parental problems
When alcohol or drugs become the prime focus of a parent's attention, or mental illness blunts perceptions, the infants may be dressed inappropriately and hygiene grossly neglected. Parental problems may inhibit the ability to care about themselves or their children. Infants who are regularly rejected come to see themselves as unloved and unlovable (Fahlberg, 1991).

Parental apathy and despair, which can result from mental illness, alcohol and drug use, or domestic violence, may hamper the ability of parents to empathise with and appropriately respond to their children's needs. The infant may develop identity problems if parents or carers call the child by a different name or if they are highly critical of the child and show little warmth.

Family and social relationships

Expected relationships

During the first six months of life babies begin to distinguish important figures in their life. Nonetheless, this is an age when most adults, even strangers, are able to comfort a distressed infant. After the age of 2 years infants become increasingly selective. The attention of strangers is likely to upset them and children generally become distressed when their attachment figure leaves them (Bowlby, 1969; Fahlberg, 1991).

Before the age of 2 years play is solitary or carried out in parallel with other children (Smith and Cowie, 1991).

The possible impact of parental problems

There are a number of ways by which the relationship between parents and children may be affected: unsettled babies may be difficult to comfort, parents' behaviour may be inconsistent, disorganised, or emotionally detached, and parents' commitment to children may be reduced.

The attachment process is influenced by both the infant and the adult. When babies are born suffering from withdrawal symptoms, their unsettled behaviour and the inability of parents to comfort them is likely to influence the nature of the bond between parent and child (Herjanic et al, 1979). These babies are at greater risk of attachment problems than other babies (Fahlberg, 1991).

Mental illness, problem alcohol or drug use, or the psychological consequences of being a victim of domestic violence can all affect the ability of a parent to maintain consistency, predictability and a physical presence in relation to the child. Research suggests mothers who experience these problems display less aptitude to provide for the baby's needs for bodily contact and loving care. Differences in the mother's response to the infant are apparent at 3 months. It has been argued that maternal insensitivity to the infant's signals will have an adverse affect on the attachment process (Svedin et al, 1996).

Research suggests depressed mothers are more disorganised, unhappy, tense and irritable than non-depressed mothers. They are shown to be less effective, show more anger and are less playful with their infants (Bettes, 1988; Field et al, 1990). These are issues key to the attachment process. A point which is reinforced by Murray's (1992) research on post-natal depression which found infants to be more insecurely attached than children of well mothers. This was despite the fact that in most cases the depression had remitted by 3 or 4 months after the child was born (Murray, 1992).

The detrimental impact on attachment of the mother's depressed mood will be compounded if she is living in a violent relationship. Rather than being able to compensate, violent fathers often emotionally distance themselves from their children (Holden and Ritchie, 1991).

When parents put their own needs above those of the infant, which may happen when parents have alcohol or drug problems or are mentally ill, this reduces their commitment and may interfere with the attachment process (Fahlberg, 1991). For example, when parents have a psychotic illness, attachment may be affected because the ill parent is guided by hallucinations which include the baby (Cassin, 1996). The hypothesis of a relationship between maternal commitment to the infant and subsequent attachment is supported by research which shows an increase of anxious attachment in children of schizophrenic mothers but not in children of mothers who suffered other types of mental illness (Naslund et al, 1984, referred to in Rutter, 1989).

Emotional and behavioural development: self-care skills

Expected development and self-care skills
'The primary task to be accomplished during the first year of life is for the baby to develop trust in others' (Fahlberg, 1991, p.64).

This is achieved when a baby's needs are regularly satisfied by a familiar carer. The major characteristics of an attachment relationship is that the presence of a person to whom the child is attached reduces the child's anxiety in stressful situations. This allows the baby to feel sufficiently confident to explore their world (Bowlby, 1969). The process of attachment is not confined to a single adult. Babies can develop secure attachments to more than one adult as long as they are constant figures in the babies' lives (Bowlby, 1969; Rutter, 1995; Thoburn, 1996).

The possible impact of parental problems
There are two main ways parents' problems may impact on babies. The infant is affected by parents' moods, and they are upset by displays of parental anger.

Babies under 12 months have little sense of self and are, therefore, very dependant on their parents or key carers for their psychological well being (Fahlberg, 1991). To a great extent the baby's emotions and subsequent behaviours are related to the moods and actions of those who are looking after them. Consequently, the depressed affect, emotional withdrawal and unpredictable mood swings that frequently accompany problem drinking or drug use, mental illness, or domestic violence may be mirrored by the infant.

Research which looks at this issue in infants offers some substantiation for the notion. Infants of depressed mothers were found to show more emotional and behavioural disturbances than children of well mothers (Cox et al, 1987). In addition, children as young as 18 months were found to become upset during angry exchanges between parents and children aged 2 years became distressed during simulated arguments (Hester and Radford, 1995). Research focusing on the impact of domestic violence suggests pre-school children may be negatively affected. Recorded symptoms included raised anxiety and fear, low self-esteem and sleep disorders (Brandon and Lewis, 1996).

To sum up

Key problems for children 0–2 years

- Drugs and alcohol use and violence during pregnancy may have caused neurological and physical damage to the baby.
- Babies may be neglected physically and emotionally to the detriment of their health.
- The child's health problems may be exacerbated by living in an impoverished physical environment.
- Cognitive development of the infant may be delayed through parents' inconsistent, under-stimulating and neglecting behaviour.
- Children may fail to develop a positive identity because they are rejected and are uncertain of who they are.
- Babies suffering withdrawal symptoms from foetal addiction may be difficult to manage.
- A lack of commitment and increased unhappiness, tension and irritability in parents may result in inappropriate responses which lead to faulty attachment.

Protective factors

- The presence of an alternative or supplementary caring adult who can respond to the developmental needs of babies.
- Sufficient income support and good physical standards in the home.
- Regular supportive help from primary health care team and social services, including consistent day care.
- An alternative, safe and supportive residence for mothers subject to violence and the threat of violence.

Children aged 3–4 years

Health

Expected health

Parents or carers need to ensure immunisations are up to date and the child's weight and height are within the normal range. Children who do not have learning or physical disabilities should be achieving their developmental milestones. Those with learning or physical disabilities should get continued professional attention. Illnesses and injuries also should be given appropriate treatment.

The possible impact of parental problems

There are several factors emanating from parental problems which may place the child's health at risk. Parents need to be in a fit state to protect the child from physical danger; children should not be left alone; their physical needs should be met; and they need to be protected from physical abuse.

Parents of pre-school children need to be in a mental state which allows them to anticipate danger and to provide feelings of safety. Depression, problem drinking and drug use however, can deprive the sufferer of the capacity to care about those whom they love (Kandal et al, 1991). This carelessness may result in children being physically at risk from drugs and needles.

When parents are problem drinkers or drug users, the desire to satisfy their own needs may mean children are placed at risk. Drugs and alcohol need to be purchased and to do this young children may be left alone at home, or with unsuitable carers.

> '...B was 3 years old. One night, S was arrested by the police for soliciting. At the station she told the police that she had left B on her own at home... S was financing her habit through prostitution. She said that her craving for crack cocaine was so overwhelming that she did not care what she did to raise the money...B was seriously underweight and had marked developmental problems, especially in language' (case example in Swadi, 1994, p.241).

This example also suggests that when parents are taken up with their own needs, ensuring that young children are adequately fed may not always be a priority.

Young children are most at risk from parental mental illness when they are the victims of aggressive acts or hostile behaviour, or are neglected or suffer parental rejection (Rutter, 1966; d'Orban, 1979; Falkov, 1996).

Education and cognitive ability

Expected ability

By the age of 4 years many children benefit from regular attendance at a pre-school facility. *'Those who have been to nursery or play group start school with several advantages: they find it easier to settle and to make friends and they are better prepared to cope with academic work'* (Department of Health, 1995b).

Most children can now concentrate well and benefit from a variety of play, drawing and writing materials. As Fahlberg aptly notes, *'Play is the work of the pre-school child'* (Fahlberg, 1991, p.73).

Although children enjoy playing by themselves they are beginning to be able to 'take turns'. Pretend play is developing and it is not unusual for pre-school children to have an imaginary friend (Smith and Cowie, 1991).

During the infant years vocabulary increases significantly. However, children need encouragement to develop language skills and should be listened to, and helped to take part in conversations. Reading to children helps them develop their knowledge and understanding of words and language.

When children's development is delayed a parent or carer should seek relevant information and professional advice. If children have little or no speech, with help they may learn to communicate non-verbally.

The possible impact of parental problems

Parental problems may have an adverse impact on the infant's cognitive development because of two factors: parents' behaviour and their social circumstances.

The conflicting findings around the impact of maternal depression on children's education and cognitive development, discussed in the section for children 0–2 years, remains unresolved in studies which focus on older infants. For example, Sharp et al's (1995) findings suggest that post-natal depression is associated with poorer intellectual development in boys at the age of 3 years 10 months, while the work of Hammen (1988) found no such relationship.

Children's cognitive development may also be affected by parental problem drinking. Research using developmental tests show deficits are apparent in pre-school children (Royal College of Physicians, 1995).

> *'Children of problem drinkers studied both in childhood and adulthood reveal cognitive deficits when compared with children of non-drinkers'* (Royal College of Physicians, 1995, p.18).

Domestic violence has also been shown to be associated with children showing a lack of interest in their environment and poorer intellectual development. A possible explanation may be that growing up in a violent household results in children being too frightened to show inquisitiveness or to attempt to explore their environment. A further interpretation of apathy and disinterest in young children, is that it indicates insecure attachments (see section on family and social relationships).

When parents are taken up with their own problems, offering educational and cognitive stimulation to children may be given scant attention. There is some evidence to suggest that depressed mothers interact less with their children than well mothers (Davenport et al, 1984).

Additionally, there may be an indirect influence. The disorganisation and torpor resulting from mental illness or problem alcohol or drug use, or the psychological consequences of domestic violence may mean that parents fail to regularly take children to nursery or other pre-school facilities. Attendance may also be affected because an abused mother may wish to conceal the evidence of domestic violence.

Finally, it has to be remembered that the impact of these types of negative parental behaviours will not affect children uniformly. The differences may be understood if we consider the more holistic approach adopted by Rutter (1989). His work looks at children as individuals and seeks to explain how they may differ in their resilience and vulnerability in the face of adversity.

Identity and social presentation

Expected identity and social presentation

Children of this age may have little understanding of race but are generally aware of their gender. Most children know who their parents and siblings are and have a sense of who belongs to their immediate family. Children can generally give their first name and last name and know how old they are.

Pre-school children are at the stage of integrating the 'good' and 'bad' aspects of self. Through adults telling them about the way they behave, children can learn that sometimes their behaviour is good, while at other times it is not. The expectation is that by integrating these two aspects of themselves they will come to believe that *'they are good people who sometimes do "not good" things'* (Fahlberg, 1991, p.74).

The possible impact of parental problems

The impact of adverse parenting for this age group is more damaging in some areas than in others. The most likely damage will result from children blaming themselves for parents' problems, taking on too much responsibility, and being physically neglected. Damage can also occur when children are included in parental hallucinations and fantasies.

As will be shown for older children, some are expected to take on responsibilities beyond their years. There are surprising examples of how even very young children see themselves as responsible for their parents' behaviour and make attempts to put things right. Reports from mothers who are victims of domestic violence suggest that infants who witness the violence try to protect their mother.

> 'He smashed my head against the wall because (the baby) was making a mess...I just collapsed on the floor. (The baby) was trying to pull me across the floor crying...saying "Mummy get up"
> (quoted in NCH, 1994).

Parents may neglect their own and their children's physical care because of their problems with drugs or alcohol, or because they are depressed. In some extreme cases the effects of parents' problems may be such that basic hygiene is neglected and children are left in a filthy condition. At this age few children are sufficiently skilled to see to their own needs.

Children living with a parent who is suffering hallucinations may be vulnerable to physical harm or emotional damage. Quinton and Rutter (1985) have suggested that drawing children into parents' fantasies may place them at risk in all areas of development, and in extreme cases this may result in the child's death (see Resnich, 1969; Gibson, 1975; Falkov, 1996).

Family and social relationships

Expected relationships and self-care skills

The fear of strangers gradually diminishes and the need to be physically near a parent is no longer so urgent. After the age of 3 years children begin to more easily understand why a parent (attachment figure) has to leave and they become less distressed by short separations. It is generally accepted that children can cope well with having more than one adult look after them, provided that they are the same care givers over time and that child and carers have a secure attachment relationship (Rutter, 1995). However, this is a fearful age: the greatest of which is a fear that parents will abandon them (Fahlberg, 1991).

Pre-school children start to establish relationships with peers and develop social skills. Research has shown that children of this age show pro-social behaviour such as sharing, helping or comforting. The development of pro-social behaviour is thought to be influenced by parental reinforcement or punishment for not being helpful (Smith and Cowie, 1991).

The possible impact of parental problems

The impact of parental mental illness, problem alcohol/drug use, or domestic violence on children of this age results from inconsistent parenting, emotional unavailability, learning to imitate inappropriate behaviour, being exposed to inappropriate carers, and separation.

Young children living in families where at least one parent has a mood disorder, or a problem with drink or drugs, or where there is domestic violence, are more likely to experience inconsistent parenting. As a result children never know what will happen or whether their needs will be met. In such situations children become fearful and unnaturally vigilant believing they are in continual danger (Davenport et al, 1984).

Another problem associated with parental mental illness, alcohol or drug misuse, or domestic violence, is that parents become unavailable emotionally. This can result in young children developing insecure attachments. Infants may respond to insecure attachments by showing apathy and disinterest in their environment. Alternatively, they may exhibit controlling behaviour which is often accompanied by a good deal of inner turmoil. Infants may cope with disturbing parental behaviours by apparently not responding. These children can appear more competent in dealing with adverse parental behaviours, but in reality they are attempting to prevent further frightening responses from the parent (Jones et al, 1991).

The third problem is that young children model their parents' behaviour. The effects of witnessing domestic violence on the behaviour of a three year old are illustrated in a case study where *'When Robert was with other children he was aggressive and violent towards them'* (Brandon and Lewis, 1996, p.37). Such findings suggest that exposure to domestic violence can result in very young children learning to resolve conflict through violence.

Neglectful parents who are preoccupied with their own needs may leave children in the care of inappropriate adults, thus exposing them to the possibility of abuse.

When parents' problems require hospitalisation or are so extreme that children need to be looked after full time by others, children of this age group are very much at risk. This is because of their inability to think beyond the immediate and the concrete. Unlike older children, the cognitive ability of children aged 3–4 years is less developed which makes it difficult for them to grasp explanations for the long term absence of a parent (see Aldgate, 1991).

Emotional and behavioural development: self-care skills

Expected development and self-care skills

Children are gradually gaining greater control over their behaviour. Temper tantrums include both verbal expressions of anger and frustration, as well as physical ones, such as biting, hitting and scratching (Fahlberg, 1991).

With maturation children normally learn to have control over bladder and bowels (Smith and Cowie, 1991).

Children are usually friendly and helpful. They have learnt to dress and undress themselves although they generally enjoy being helped.

This is an age when children are plagued with irrational fears, for example many are frightened of the dark or of loud noises (Fahlberg, 1991). However, as mentioned earlier, the main fear of children is that of abandonment, perhaps not so irrational in today's world (see Owusu-Bempah, 1995, 1997 for a discussion of this).

The possible impact of parental problems

This age group are very vulnerable to the development of emotional and behavioural disturbance and may regress in their behaviour. When children of this age become frightened of their parents' behaviour fears may build up, and children may be at increasing risk because they cannot easily articulate their emotions.

There is considerable evidence to suggest that children of depressed mothers show more emotional and behavioural disturbances (see for example Cox et al, 1987; Caplan et al, 1989). Although some observational studies suggest this may reflect the mother's negative perceptions of her child rather than real differences in behaviour (Lang et al, 1996), work by Glaser et al (1997) found parental mental illness to be associated with emotional abuse.

When parents' behaviour is unpredictable and frightening, which can be the result of mental illness or problem alcohol/drug use, or domestic violence, research suggests children react with symptoms similar to those identified in post-traumatic stress disorder. These include sleep disturbance, bed-wetting and rocking (see Juliana and Goodman, 1997 with reference to substance abuse; Brandon and Lewis, 1996 with reference to domestic violence; and Rutter, 1989 for effects of mental illness).

Extreme anxiety and fear may also result from children seeing their parents as powerless or untrustworthy. They may react by withdrawing or alternatively by always trying to please (Falhberg, 1991). These symptoms are noted in the National Children's Home (1994) study of children who experience domestic violence. Many mothers talked about their children's fear. *'They would wake up screaming and crying'* (NCH, 1994, p.35).

Practically two thirds of mothers mentioned other disturbing reactions. Children feared any type of separation, *'She would be very clingy, and even followed me to the toilet',* others were unnaturally quiet or withdrawn, while over a third developed bed-wetting problems (NCH, 1994, p.35). Children who both witnessed violence directed towards their mother, and had been the direct victims of violence, experienced significantly more behavioural problems than those who had only witnessed the violence or had not witnessed or been a victim (Hughes, 1988).

Pre-school children may be more at risk of emotional disturbance than older more articulate children because they are less able to express their distress verbally (Brandon and Lewis, 1996). Moreover, the extent of their distress can be missed because young children's observable reaction may not tally with their emotional state.

> *'It may in fact take some time before children are able to show any reaction at all but this should not be taken to mean that the child has been unaffected by the violence'* (McGee, 1997, p.19).

To sum up

Key problems for children 3–4 years

- Children are placed in physical danger by parents whose physical capacity to care is limited by mental illness, excessive drinking or drug use, or domestic violence.

- Children may have their physical needs neglected, for example, they may be unfed and unwashed.

- Children may be subjected to direct physical violence by parents.

- Children's cognitive development may be delayed through lack of stimulation, disorganisation and failure to attend pre-school facilities.

- Children's attachment may be damaged by inconsistent parenting.

- Children may learn inappropriate behavioural responses through witnessing domestic violence.

- When parents behaviour is unpredictable and frightening children may display emotional symptoms similar to those of post-traumatic stress disorder.

- Children may take on responsibilities beyond their years because of parental incapacity.

- Children may be at risk because they are unable to tell anybody about their distress.

Protective factors

- The presence of an alternative, consistent caring adult who can respond to the cognitive and emotional needs of the child.

- Sufficient income support and good physical standards in the home.

- Regular supportive help to the family from primary health care team and social services, including consistent day care, respite care, accommodation and family assistance.

- Regular attendance at pre-school facilities.

- An alternative, safe and supportive residence for mothers subject to violence and the threat of violence.

Children aged 5–9 years

Health

Expected health

Children aged 5–9 years should have regular medical and dental examinations, either through the school medical or with the family doctor and dentist. These check-ups should ensure that the child's height and weight are within normal limits, and that problems with hearing and sight, physical dexterity and mobility are identified and addressed. Although children's co-ordination is improving, at 5 and 6 years they frequently over-estimate their ability and injure themselves during normal play. Convulsions are rare at this age unless associated with high fevers or a recognised physical condition.

At this age children with no speech or hearing problems and who are not learning disabled should have a well developed vocabulary and communicate easily with adults and children.

When there is a permanent hearing loss or physical disability which interferes with verbal communication, children should be communicating using a form of signing. Children with physical disabilities are increasingly able to understand their condition and talk about it. Many children with disabilities take part in specialised group activities.

The possible impact of parental problems

There are two issues with relation to children's health. An increased risk of physical injury, and extreme anxiety and fear.

Children whose parents suffer from mental illness or who have a violent relationship with their intimate partner, have an increased risk of medical problems, including injuries, convulsive disorders and, like the children of parents with alcohol problems, increased frequency of hospitalisation (see Weissman et al, 1986 for parental mental illness; Cork, 1969, Brisby et al, 1997 for problem drinking, and for domestic violence see Farmer and Owen 1995; Moffitt and Caspi, 1998). The link between domestic violence and physical child abuse is illustrated by Moffitt and Caspi (1998).

> 'Among parents who engaged in serious spouse abuse, half of the fathers and a quarter of the mothers said they had also engaged in serious child abuse' (Moffitt and Caspi, 1998, p.142).

Living with carers who have a violent relationship or who have a drink problem is also associated with children showing a number of other health related issues, many which would be considered psychosomatic symptoms of anxiety. These include, stomach pains, headaches, asthma, enuresis, allergies, disturbed sleep patterns and headaches (for domestic violence see Carroll, 1994; for issues related to problem alcohol use see Cork, 1969; Lewis and Bucholz, 1991).

Children's health problems may go unrecognised because school absenteeism as a result of parenting problems may mean school medicals are missed.

Education and cognitive ability

Expected ability

The normal child attends school regularly and on the whole enjoys the experience. Teachers are generally liked and most children have at least one friend.

Children of 5 and 6 years frequently aspire to do more than they can achieve and easily become frustrated. There is an increasing ability to concentrate as children are able to screen out distractions and focus on a single issue.

By 9 years children are capable of long periods of concentration. They should be proficient in school subjects, able to read, use basic maths and write.

Notions of truth and fairness are increasingly understood.

The possible impact of parental problems

The issues for children of this age relate to: academic attainment, and behaviour in school.

When exploring the impact of parental mental illness, problem alcohol or drug use, or domestic violence on children's cognitive ability and educational attainments the evidence is somewhat contradictory. This lack of clarity pertains to research findings in relation to both parental mental illness and problem drinking.

For example, some studies have suggested that post-natal depression is associated with a negative impact on children's cognitive development. A comparison of 5–6 year old children of hospitalised schizophrenic and depressed women and a control group found the children whose mothers were depressed showed most failures on tests of attention and greatest impairment in intellectual ability (Cohler et al, 1977). Similarly, Sharp et al (1995) noted a significant cognitive impairment in boys of mothers who had suffered post-natal depression. Further evidence comes from Weissman et al (1986) who noted that teachers reported children of depressed mothers to be more likely to require special educational classes than those whose mothers were not depressed.

However, Murray et al (1996) suggests that the negative impact of maternal mental illness on the child's cognition is due to the combined effect of post-natal depression and social adversity. Post-natal depression in relatively low risk populations was shown to have no long-term negative affect on children's intellectual ability at age five.

Research findings on the association between children's cognitive development and education and parental alcohol and drug misuse generally suggest a moderately negative effect. For example, out of nine studies exploring the relation between parents with problem drinking and children's IQ, six found children had significantly lower scores. Other research focused on academic performance in school and out of six studies, five reported the children of alcoholics to have a significantly lower performance (reviewed in West and Prinz, 1987). Similar results have been found for the children of heroin addicted fathers (see Hogan, 1998 for a review of this literature).

The second problem area is that of child's behaviour in school. Emery et al (1982) found that parental schizophrenia was associated with problematic school behaviour in children. The same direct relationship was not obtained in cases of maternal depression unless marital discord was also present.

In the area of domestic violence there is less evidence concerning the impact on children's cognitive development. However, in a study of 28 maritally violent couples with 66 children, 45% of 7 year old boys displayed aggression and anxiety, whilst 37% of the girls were under-achieving in school (Moore et al 1979, quoted in Gough, 1993).

Identity

Expected identity

Children of this age see themselves as autonomous and separate individuals from their parents. In general they are at ease with themselves and accept their gender, race and physical attributes. They expect to be liked by both peers and adults, and see adults as dependable and trustworthy (Smith and Cowie, 1991).

The family is valued and the child knows important members. Their own history intrigues them and there is an interest in photos and stories from earlier years (Fahlberg, 1991).

Magical and egocentric thinking characterise this age. Children believe that wishes and ritualised behaviour can make things happen (Fahlberg, 1991).

The possible impact of parental problems

For this age group there are three issues with regard to the impact of parental problems on the child's developing identity: gender, self-esteem, and guilt.

There is some evidence to suggest that gender may influence the children's ability to cope with parental problems. Being of the same gender as a parent who has problems appears to be more traumatising and psychologically distressing than for children of the opposite sex (for domestic violence see Fantuzzo and Lindquist, 1989, for mental illness see Rutter and Quinton, 1984).

Self-esteem is another problem. There is evidence to suggest that children falling into this age bracket who live with a mentally ill parent have a more negative self-image and poorer self-esteem than their peers. Svedin et al's (1996) longitudinal study of 156 pregnant women found that by the age of 8 years, children of mothers categorised as 'mentally insufficient' (this included both psychiatric illness and learning disabilities) were faring less well than children in the reference group.

The research on the impact on children of parents with drink problems or who live with parents who are violent towards one another suggests that children may be at risk of developing low self-esteem and a belief that they are unable to control events in their environment.

'My father did not let me sit on the sofa with my brother, I had to sit on the floor. When he got angry he held my head in the

toilet' (a 7 year old boy describing his experiences to a Women's Aid refuge worker, Greenwich Asian Women's Project, 1996).

However, West and Prinz (1987) reviewed the research on the impact of parental problem drinking and found that there was considerable inconsistency between the research designs and that in some research the effects could not be attributed directly to parents' problem drinking.

A third problem is that children may assume they are responsible for their parents' actions. It is commonly reported that children of problem drinking parents, or whose parents are violent to each other (see Emery, 1982; Saunders et al, 1995), feel that they are somehow at fault for what is happening. Children may believe that what they do triggers their parents' drinking or violence, or that they should be able to find a way of stopping it. Younger children's description of the ways they have tried to stop their parents from drinking in many cases include, *'methods containing a magical element, for example finding exactly the right words'* (Brisby et al, 1997, p.11).

Doyle's recollection of his violent childhood illustrates a belief in the magical quality of words.

> *'People were talking, kind of shouting. I stopped. It was cold...*
> *The television was on; that meant my Ma and Da weren't in bed. They were still downstairs. It wasn't burglars in the kitchen...*
> *- Stop.*
> *I only whispered it.*
> *For a while I thought it was only Da, shouting in the way people did when they were trying not to, but sometimes forgot; a bit like screamed whispers...*
> *But Ma was shouting as well...*
> *I did it again.*
> *- Stop.*
> *There was a gap. It had worked; I'd forced them to stop'*

(Doyle, R. 1994, p.42.)

The extent to which children blame themselves for parents' problems seems to depend on parents' ability to help children recognise that the problems lie with the adults themselves rather than with the child. Hill et al (1996) looked at children's accounts of living with drinking parents and found little evidence of children blaming themselves for their parents' drinking problems. It could be argued that because children of this age generally interpret the effects of alcohol or drugs in terms of illness, it is easier for them to accept and adjust to the consequences (Rutter, 1990).

Family and social relationships

Expected relations

Children enjoy physical closeness and generally have a confiding relationship with a parent. They may have difficulty talking about their feelings, and find it easier to discuss them in retrospect.

Children have developed the ability to understand time which means they can cope well with short separations from a parent.

Peers are increasingly important and friends are valued for their physical attributes. At this age children develop the ability to put themselves in the shoes of others and understand the impact their behaviour may have on other people. As a result children are able to sustain friendships and to function within a group (Hartup, 1983). Friendships have been shown to play a very supportive role and children with a friend suffer less loneliness than those without (Dunn and McGuire, 1992).

The possible impact of parental problems

The main problems for children are: inconsistent parental behaviour which may cause anxiety and faulty attachments, fear of hostility, and unplanned separation. Children feel helpless and guilty in cases of domestic violence. Some assume a role beyond their years.

A major problem for children is that mental illness, problem alcohol or drug use, or the psychological consequences of domestic violence can cause parents to behave in inconsistent and unexpected ways. This is difficult for children to understand, and as one nine year old boy said to his problem drinking mother *'I didn't know whether you loved me'* (quoted in Brisby et al, 1997, p.14).

A second issue for children is the fear, guilt and helplessness in the face of parental violence. Research has shown that in some cases of domestic violence male perpetrators insist children witness their mothers' abuse (Hamner, 1989; Jaffe et al, 1990; Hestor and Radford, 1996). Children, even at this young age, may try to protect or look after the parent. For example, they may call the police or doctor, adopt a caring role, or mediate between warring parents (Dobash and Dobash, 1984; Hamner, 1989). *'At the age of eight I became like my daddy's wife, not in a sexual way but in all the other things'* (quoted in Brisby et al, 1997, p.14)

Parental mental illness is also associated with increased levels of hostility for children of this age. Research shows that depressed mothers show greater hostility in their inter-action with school aged children than younger ones. Panaccione and Wahler (1986) found a strong association between the mothers' depressive symptoms and hostile child directed behaviour which included shouting and slapping.

The child's fear may also be the result of anticipated hostility. In situations of domestic violence, mothers and children may find that the everyday aspects of their lives are subjected to a frightening and pervasive control.

> *'We wasn't allowed down in the front room at all, we had to stay in our bedrooms, we had to stay, the only time we could come out was when we eat'* (9 year old boy quoted in McGee, 1996).

Finally, there is the impact on children when separation from an attachment figure is unavoidable. Because children of this age have a greater understanding of time, they are less likely to show the high levels of distress expected from younger children. *'Nonetheless, if parents' departure seems capricious, unexplained, unacceptable or frightening in context, separation anxiety will be manifest'* (Rutter and Rutter, 1992, p.113).

Social presentation

Expected presentation

Children of this age generally appear well cared for and are appropriately dressed. Children can make themselves understood by people outside the family and many of those without verbal ability have begun to use a form of non-verbal communication.

In general the child has learnt appropriate social skills and can adjust their behaviour and conversation to suit an increasingly wide range of situations, for example peers, teachers and family.

The possible impact of parental problems

Mental illness, problem drinking or drug use or domestic violence can cause children shame and embarrassment. Karr (1995) describes the shame experienced by a 6 year old girl whose parents were violent towards one another.

> *'I felt like the neighbours' stares had bored so many imaginary holes in our walls that the whole house was rotten as wormy wood. I never quite got over thinking that folks looked at us funny on mornings after Mother and Daddy had fought'* (Karr, 1995, p.39).

Children want to belong to ordinary families. When parents' problems lead them to behave in unpredictable or embarrassing ways children want to keep it secret. The description in Deane's book of his early childhood experiences of living with a mentally ill mother, offers a touching description of such childhood anxiety.

'*We were all frightened. Also, I was ashamed. When I saw her wandering around the house, touching the walls, tracing out the scrolls of varnish on the sitting-room door with her finger, or climbing wearily up the stairs to gaze out of the window, my cheeks burnt and the semi-darkness seemed to be full of eyes. She was going out from us, becoming strange, becoming possessed, and I didn't want anyone else outside the family to know or notice*' (Deane, 1996, pp.140–141).

A consequence of this wish to keep the family's distress and disintegration hidden is that children are more fearful and less willing to risk social encounters. Friendships and social inter-action are restricted.

Emotional and behavioural development

Expected development

Children trust and confide in adults and seek comfort from them when distressed.

Children aged 5 and 6 years are frequently very active with a poor ability to modulate their behaviour. Concepts of ownership are not yet fully established and it is not uncommon for 6 year olds to happily take things that belong to others. For example, children in infant school may come home having 'found' pencils or small toys.

Children of 5 and 6 years frequently revert to behaviours normal for earlier years – sucking thumb, communicating through baby talk etc. When children are frustrated, temper tantrums involve name calling which often is lavatorial in nature. Cruelty to animals is not uncommon (Falhberg, 1991).

By the age of 8 and 9 years family values become incorporated and the child increasingly relies on internal, as opposed to external, controls. For example, the child's behaviour is no longer entirely dependant upon the immediate presence of an adult. When frustrated or angry it is not uncommon, particularly in boys, to talk of fighting and 'beating up' other children. Actual aggression though is more likely to be verbal rather than physical. Swearing shifts from elimination-related words to a vocabulary associated with sex.

The possible impact of parental problems

There are several ways that parental problems can have an adverse affect on the emotions and behaviour of children aged 5–9 years. Children show their distress through conduct disorders and emotional distress, uncontrolled behaviour and fear.

Children may cope with the stress produced by unpredictable, unexpected and irrational parental behaviour by seeking to escape.

They may do this through fantasy and make-believe, where the frightening behaviour of their parents is reinterpreted in acceptable ways.

> *'Sometimes, when my parents were raging at each other in the kitchen, Lecia and I would talk about finding a shack on the beach to live in. We'd sit cross-legged under the blue cotton quilt with a flashlight, doing parodies of their fights. "Reel Six, Tape Fifty One. Let her roll," Lecia would say...as if what we were listening to was only one more take in a long movie we were shooting'* (Karr, 1995, p.38).

As with identity, the impact of parental problems on children's behaviour depends on their gender and temperament. Research shows that boys are initially more vulnerable to the ill effects of living with a parent suffering mental illness or in a situation of family violence. But if adverse family circumstances continue long enough girls are also likely to succumb (Rutter, 1985).

Gender may also influence the way children react to adversity. It is widely accepted that boys are more likely to act out their distress with anti-social and aggressive behaviours such as stealing, lying, attention seeking, and attacks on peers. In contrast, girls tend to respond by internalising their worries, showing symptoms of depression, anxiety and withdrawal (Bentovim and Williams, 1998). For information on gender differences with regard to parental mental illness see for example Rutter and Quinton (1984), for domestic violence see Morley and Mullender (1994) and Mullender et al (1998), for drug use see Greco-Vigorito et al (1996). However, regardless of gender, parental drinking problems tend to lead children to externalise their distress – conduct problems, restlessness and inattention, and poor academic performance are noted reactions (West and Prinz, 1987; Velleman, 1993).

Temperament of the child is also an issue. When parents became irritable, aggressive and quarrelsome this does not impinge equally on all children in the family. Research has suggested that parental annoyance is most likely to be directed towards the temperamentally 'difficult' child (Rutter and Quinton, 1984).

There are several behavioural and emotional problems associated with children exposed to parents with extreme problems. Downey and Coyne's (1990) comprehensive review of the literature on the children of depressed parents concludes that school aged children generally show higher levels of problem behaviours than control children.

There is considerable dispute, however, over how children manifest their problems. Work by Hammen et al (1978), Beardsley et al (1987) and Klein et al (1988) all found a significantly higher rate of conduct disorder in children of depressed parents. In contrast, Lee and Gotlib

(1989) found maternal depression was related to emotional disorders in children aged 7–12, such as greater fear and mood disturbances, but failed to show an association between maternal depression and conduct disorders in children. Emotional and behaviour problems were likely to continue after maternal depression abated (Billings and Moos, 1985; Lee and Gotlib, 1989).

A further important factor is that children who witness anger or violence have been shown to have problems in controlling their emotions and behaviour (Cicchetti and Toth, 1995). Temper tantrums, aggression or extreme passivity with sudden outbursts are the frequently recorded behaviours of children living in situations of domestic violence (Brandon and Lewis, 1996). For example, they quote a paediatric nurse's comments about a 6–year old,

> *'I've seen her very upset on the ward literally running up the curtains when her father got violent on the ward'* (Brandon and Lewis, 1996, p.61).

Another illustration comes from Mary Karr who describes growing up with parents who drank to excess and were violent to each other:

> *'And Lecia and I both behaved like savages at any opportunity...I can remember standing behind the drainage ditch in our yard cussing Carol Sharp for bloodying my nose. I had blood sprayed down the front of my new yellow sunsuit, one that tied at the shoulders and had elastic around the legs. I couldn't have been more than six, but I was calling her an ignorant little bitch'* (Karr, 1995, p.40).

Finally, research which includes the accounts of children of this age range gives clear evidence of the fear and anxiety which these parental issues can generate. The accounts of two children, who live with problem drinking parents, speak for themselves:

> *'I was scared that mummy would kill herself with the drink'* (Brisby et al, 1997, p.14).

> *'I was scared that my daddy would leave'* (Brisby et al, 1997, p.14).

Self-care skills

Expected self-care skills

Children of this age will be able to help adults or older siblings with household chores. Similarly, children are able to help look after younger siblings or assist in the care of sick or disabled parents. However, children of this age are too young to adequately shoulder the parental role and an adult should always retain responsibility for their own and their children's care.

The possible impact of parental problems

The problems for this age group are that children may be expected to take too much responsibility for themselves. Moreover, because of parents' inconsistent and neglecting behaviour they may have to assume a parenting role (ChildLine, 1997).

> *'Sam (9 years) took responsibility for protecting their mother from assaults by telephoning the police from a public call box, or by shouting until the neighbours came to help'* (a case study of domestic violence, quoted in Brandon and Lewis, 1996).

To sum up

Key problems for children 5–9 years

- Children may be at increased risk of physical injury, and show symptoms of extreme anxiety and fear.
- Academic attainment is negatively affected and children's behaviour in school becomes problematic.
- Identity, age and gender may affect outcomes. Boys more quickly exhibit problematic behaviour but girls are also affected if parental problems endure.
- Children may develop poor self-esteem, and may blame themselves for their parents' problems.
- Inconsistent parental behaviour may cause anxiety and faulty attachments.
- Children's fear of hostility.
- Unplanned separation can cause distress and disrupt education and friendship patterns.
- Children feel embarrassment and shame over parents' behaviour. As a consequence they curtail friendships and social inter-action.
- Children may take on too much responsibility for themselves, their parents and younger siblings.

Protective factors

- Children have the cognitive ability to rationalise drug and alcohol problems in terms of illness. This enables them to accept and cope with parents' behaviour more easily.
- The presence of an alternative, consistent, caring adult who can respond to the cognitive and emotional needs of children.
- Sufficient income support and good physical standards in the home.

- Regular supportive help from a primary health care team and social services, including respite care and accommodation.

- Regular attendance at school.

- Sympathetic, empathic and vigilant teachers.

- Attendance at school medicals.

- An alternative, safe and supportive residence for mothers subject to violence and the threat of violence.

- A supportive older sibling. Older siblings can offer significant support to children particularly when parents are overwhelmed by their own problems (Kosonen, 1996).

- A friend. Children who have at least one mutual friend have been shown to have higher self worth and lower scores on loneliness than those without (Parker and Asher, 1992, quoted in Stocker, 1994).

- Social networks outside the family, especially with a sympathetic adult of the same sex.

- Belonging to organised out-of-school activities, including homework clubs.

- Being taught different ways of coping and being sufficiently confident to know what to do when parents are incapacitated.

- An ability to separate, either psychologically or physically from the stressful situation. This has been shown to act as a protective factor (see Anthony, 1974 with regard to mental illness; Velleman for alcohol misuse; Holden and Ritchie, 1991 for domestic violence).

Children aged 10–14 years

Health

Expected health

Children should have regular medical and dental checks. Immunisations need to be up to date. BCG for all those at risk of tuberculosis and immunisation against rubella for girls.

The body changes which take place at this age can confuse and distress children. For example, some girls dislike the changes puberty brings and seek to reverse them through dieting. However, most children generally eat a sufficiently balanced diet to ensure their physical development.

Puberty also brings an increase in male sex hormones which stimulates the sex drive in both genders. Between the ages of 10–14 years some children experiment with their first sexual encounter. Children need accurate factual knowledge about puberty, sex and contraception. Data on teenage pregnancy suggests a rate of 9.5 per 1000 girls aged 13–15 in 1989 (Royal College of General Practitioners, 1996).

Other types of experimentation are also common. For example, by the age of 13 some 90% of young people in England and Wales have had an alcoholic drink. For most this is only on special occasions, but some 12% own up to drinking at least once a week (Walker, 1995).

Smoking is also on the increase. Although at 11 years only 25% of children have smoked tobacco this figure steadily increases and by 14 years 60% of youngsters have tried smoking, and 17% admit being regular smokers (Office of Population and Censuses and Surveys 1995).

Drug use at this age is not common, *'three per cent of the 12 and 13 year olds questioned claimed to have taken drugs (1% for cannabis)'*. Solvents are the most commonly used substances (Baker and Marsden, 1994, p.29).

Accidental physical injuries among this age group are commonplace because many children participate in sports and physical activities.

Children with permanent hearing loss or physical disability which interferes with verbal communication should be using a form of signing. Those who have a health condition need information about it and opportunities to talk about how it affects them.

The possible impact of parental problems

There are several ways in which children's health may be affected by their parents' problems. The first is that youngsters have to cope with puberty without support. Second, there is an increased risk of psychological problems. Third, there is a risk of physical abuse and neglect. Children are actually being hurt or fear being hurt, or are anxious about how to compensate for the physical neglect they are suffering.

The first issue is that youngsters may be left to cope alone with the physical changes which accompany the onset of puberty. The emotional unavailability which can accompany parental mental illness, problem drinking and drug use, or domestic violence may mean parents are unaware of children's worries about their changing bodies. Moreover, parents may be so absorbed in their own problems that little attention is given to ensure that children attend routine medical and dental appointments.

If children have a depressed parent this can increase the risk of psychological problems. Research shows an association between parental depression and psychological symptoms in adolescents, including emotional problems, school related difficulties, suicidal behaviour and depression. The risk of major depression at this age increases linearly if both parents are psychiatrically ill compared to only one or neither parent having a psychiatric illness (Weissman et al, 1984).

A further problem is children's fear of being hurt. One of the main concerns that children expressed when parents drink to excess or are violent towards each other, is the fear of physical assault. Three out of five children with a problem drinking father and two out of five with a problem drinking mother, spoke of their own physical abuse (ChildLine, 1997). A non-drinking parent may not always be able to protect the child, because the parent who has the alcohol problem may assault both the child and the non-drinking parent.

> *'Dad gets drunk every day, he hits me and Mum...we don't pro-voke him...he broke my arm once'* (Tracy (12) quoted in ChildLine, 1997 p. 23).

Children may suffer physical abuse because they are routinely left in the care of the drinking parent.

> *'Mum works at night. Dad comes home drunk and beats me up. I dread the nights'* (Jane (12) quoted in ChildLine, 1997, p31).

In situations of domestic violence children may get injured when they try to protect one parent from the other.

> *'Joanne (13) said that her mum's partner hits her mum all the time. The last time it happened Joanne went to help her mum but she was also beaten'* (quoted in ChildLine, 1997, p35).

Finally, children may have considerable anxiety about how to compensate for the physical neglect they are experiencing. Research shows that when parents' problem drinking or drug use absorbs most of the family's income, children are fearful that they will go without basic necessities such as food and clothing (ChildLine, 1997).

Education and cognitive ability

Expected education

Most parents recognise the importance of education and school attendance. Their commitment is reflected in attending school events such as parents' evenings and meetings. The majority of children attend school regularly. Unauthorised absence is unusual at this age. The DfEE offers only global data on unauthorised absence. For secondary school children in England the proportion of half days of unauthorised absence was 1% during 1995–96. This represents an average of 21 half days unauthorised absence for each absent pupil. Less current but more specific data is given in the National Child Development Study which recorded rates of 1.2 per cent for non-school attendance among eleven year olds (cited in Carlen et al, 1992).

GCSE options are generally chosen during year 9 and course work started by year 10. Homework is the norm and children need encouragement, relative quiet and a suitable place to study. When the children's school work is not commensurate with their ability or there are other school related problems, most parents or carers take appropriate action. Parents and teachers are usually aware if a child has special educational needs and ensure the relevant resources are available.

Bullying is not uncommon at this age. A large self report survey suggests a fifth of children aged 7–12 years are occasionally, and 6% are regularly, bullied. Eight per cent of children of this age reported bullying others occasionally and 1.7% admitted to regular bullying (Smith and Thompson, 1991).

Learning does not only take place at school. Many children are involved in outside school activities, such as football, boxing, swimming, playing a musical instrument.

The possible impact of parental problems

The negative impact of parental mental illness, problem alcohol or drug use, or domestic violence on youngsters' education results from three issues: an inability to concentrate, performing below their expected ability, and missing school because of looking after parents or siblings.

The impact on children's education and academic competence is varied. For many children school is seen as a source of help or as a sanctuary from problems at home (Department of Health, 1997c). For this group school is the one area of their lives which is 'normal' and academic achievement is viewed as an escape route.

For others education is impaired because family problems preoccupy the child's thinking.

> *'I can't get on with my work at school because I'm always think-*
> *ing about what's going on at home...Mum drinks and Dad left'*
> (Sam (11) quoted in ChildLine, 1997 p37).

Brandon and Lewis (1996) found a similar fixation among children who had witnessed domestic violence. Additionally, Downey and Coyne (1990) found that children of depressed parents function at school below their expected ability.

Education may also be interrupted because children must stay at home to look after a sick or incapable parent or younger siblings (Aldridge and Becker, 1993).

> *'Anthony said that he is left to look after his baby brother. He hasn't been*
> *to school all week'* (quoted in ChildLine, 1996, p. 24).

Forty two per cent of young carers of secondary school age are missing school or have educational problems (Dearden and Becker,

1995). Many young carers believe that looking after a parent has meant they have lost opportunities for learning and as a consequence their horizons have been limited (Edwards and Smith, 1997).

Identity

Expected identity

As children enter adolescence they frequently question the belief system with which they were brought up. Although, generally, the child remains strongly identified with the values of the family (see Rutter et al, 1976) new models, provided by a more diverse group such as teachers and peers, become increasingly important. With the psychological separation from parents it is likely that family rules, values and expectations will be temporarily opposed. Although at times children can be rebellious and moody they still have a strong need to belong to the family and to be taken seriously (Fahlberg, 1991).

Most children remain integrated within the family culture and participate in important family events. Key relatives are generally known and the child understands the make-up of their family and their place in it.

Generally children are aware of and feel comfortable about their race and ethnic background.

The possible impact of parental problems

Children's attitudes and behaviours are shaped by their families. Problems for children result from them rejecting their families and low self-esteem.

Parents and close relatives act as role models and their values and beliefs are absorbed. Because this is an age when children begin to question their parents' values and beliefs, rigid family thinking or extreme behaviours such as domestic violence may lead to wholesale rejection. Research on the impact of parental drinking on children indicates that extreme parental behaviour and attitudes, whether vigorous abstinence or excessive drinking, may result in children adopting a similarly extreme but opposite pattern (Orford and Velleman, 1990; Velleman, 1993).

When parental problems take precedence within the family, children may have a poor self-image and low self-esteem. As with younger children, young teenagers may blame themselves for their parents' alcohol or drug use, or domestic violence (Herjanic et al, 1979 Rivinus, 1991; Rubio–Stipec et al, 1991).

*'When like if we'd do something bad, like we didn't take care of
our trainers or our clothes that he'd bought us, he'd take it out on
her'* (13 year old boy quoted in McGee, 1996).

Finally, the problems of being a young carer may affect children's
self-esteem. Those who take on the role of carer often feel stigmatised.
They believe they get little recognition, praise or respect for their
contribution either from parents or other adults outside the family
(Aldridge and Becker, 1993).

Family and social relationships

Expected relationships

Early adolescence is a stage when the child starts to gain a degree of
autonomy and independence. Time is increasingly spent with friends
and most children have at least one 'best friend'. Children of this age
have the ability to empathise with others and friends are valued for
their personal characteristics rather than solely for their physical attributes.

But independence takes time to accomplish and the self-assured
young teenager quickly dissolves into childish tears and temper tantrums when things don't go according to plan. This see-sawing of
emotions can take its toll on relationships with parents. At times these
may be turbulent, but regardless of the stage of independence, young
teenagers need a caring parent who understands them, offers unqualified love and allows them to retreat into childhood when necessary.

Samantha (quoted by Fahlberg 1991) provides a good illustration of
the stresses which are frequently involved in parent-child relationships
at this stage.

*'Fourteen-year-old Samantha and her mum have a fairly normal
relationship. Occasionally, when Sam's mother has been very supportive of her daughter's feelings, the teenager comments, "You are
the best mum in the world. You understand everything". Mum
replies, "I'm glad I'm doing a good job, Mums of fourteen-year-
olds are supposed to be understanding". However, just as frequently, when Mum sets limits that her daughter does not like,
Sam will scream, "you don't understand anything". Calmly
Mum responds, "I'm glad I'm doing a good job. Mothers of four-
teen-year-olds aren't supposed to understand everything"*
(Fahlberg, 1991, p.111).

The possible impact of parental problems

Parental problems can affect every aspect of family functioning.
Relationships with parents are poor. Parents are unreliable. Children

are cautious of exposing family life to outside scrutiny and as a result friendships are restricted. Children fear the family will be broken up. Isolation leaves children fearing they have no one to turn to.

Children's accounts of living with parents with alcohol problems exemplify the paucity of relationships and their unreliability (for maternal depression see Weissman et al, 1972, and Caplan et al, 1989; for problem drinking see ChildLine, 1996).

> *'Conflict and threats were commonplace, and love or warmth too often given in a drunken haze and felt to be intrusive and unreliable'* (ChildLine, 1996, p.32).

The consequence of this unreliability is that children are cautious of exposing their family life to outside scrutiny. Parents who drink excessively or have a problem with drugs can become a source of embarrassment or shame (Herjanic et al, 1979; Rivinus, 1991; Rubio-Stipec et al, 1991). As a result children feel unable to bring friends home, wanting to keep their situation secret and fearing the state their parent might be in (Brisby et al, 1997). This means that friendships are curtailed or restricted. Jan (11) talks of the shame and embarrassment caused by her mother's drinking:

> *'I had friends round one time and she came downstairs naked. All my friends make fun of me at school now'* (quoted in ChildLine, 1997, p.25).

Alternatively, the silence about family difficulties may be self-imposed or children and parents collude to keep the family secret. In many instances children fear that if their family problems become known their situation will deteriorate. A common fear is that the family will be broken up, or that people will reject them.

> *'I didn't want to tell anyone because I was afraid of what social services would do'* (child's view reported in the Brisby study, 1997, p.14).

Finally, isolation from peers, extended family or outsiders may be imposed by a parent.

> *'He says that if we ever tell anyone he will kill us...I'm scared ...it's getting worse'* (Tracy (12) whose father drank and was violent, quoted in ChildLine, 1997, p.23).

Children may cope with the stress of parental neglect or violence by running away. Many children in these circumstances have started the pattern of going missing from home by the age of 11 years. Although some stay with friends or relatives a small proportion of children aged 10–14 sleep rough. Children who wander the streets are shown to be very much at risk of detachment from school and involvement in crime (Wade and Biehal, 1998).

The isolation, whether self-imposed or due to parental threats, can leave young carers in a particularly vulnerable position. Edwards and Smith (1997) in their study reported that young carers felt there was nobody there for them and that professionals were working exclusively with the adults. They wanted someone to listen to their experiences and understand their difficulties.

Social presentation

Expected presentation

Physical appearance becomes increasingly important. Much time is spent in front of the mirror scrutinising the changes which puberty has brought. Children become very conscious about their appearance, want to choose their own clothes and their hair style, and are sensitive to criticism, particularly from peers. Children without handicapping disabilities are able to look after their own personal hygiene.

Children can communicate easily with both adults and peers and are able to regulate their language and non verbal behaviour to be appropriate to the situation.

The possible impact of parental problems

There are two major issues for this age group: the stigma and bullying which may result from the consequences of physical neglect, and learnt inappropriate behaviour such as violence, bullying and sexual abuse.

The first problem described is that of physical neglect.

> *'She described their home as being cold and dirty. They did not have hot water or any food at home'* (10 year old's experience described to Swadi, 1994, p.239).

Perhaps equally important is the stigma associated with neglect. This may be acutely felt by children of this age because they are self-conscious about their appearance and sensitive to how others see them. When parental drinking or drug use diverts monies which would ordinarily be used for household essentials and clothes, children may find it difficult to keep up an acceptable appearance and friendships may be jeopardised.

> *'They spend all the money on drink. There's no soap in the house and all my clothes are too small. I lost my girlfriend because she said I smell. Others call me names and make fun of me. It hurts'* (Paul (14) quoted in ChildLine, 1997, p.37).

The second problem results from children not learning the accepted social skills of inter-action with adults outside the family. Growing up in families where violence is an accepted way of dealing with problems can result in some children using violent or aggressive language or behaviour towards peers and adults. When children are unable to deal successfully with teachers this results in negative interactions and reinforces learning deficits and feelings of alienation (Gray, 1993).

Emotional and behavioural development

Expected development

Typical 10 and 11 year olds are emotionally unstable. '*They can fly into a rage at short notice and burst out laughing with little provocation*' (Fahlberg, 1991, p.102). There may be considerable strife with parents but on the whole they are loved and trusted. Adults in general are viewed as trustworthy.

Children may assert themselves by talking back to parents, or striking out physically or by throwing things. As children get older verbal responses become more frequent. Thirteen year olds have greater control over their emotions and can appear undemonstrative. Physical responses to anger are less common, and increasingly the child resorts to swearing, name calling and sarcasm. Although the teenage years are assumed to be a period of heightened stress, only some 7% of the population for this age range show behaviour which would be classified as disordered (Rutter et al, 1976; Cazdin, 1990).

Leaving children of any age in the sole care of older children under the age of 16 is strongly discouraged in Britain. Nonetheless in many families older siblings occasionally look after the younger brothers and sisters. Research from Scandinavian countries suggests some 70% of young children with older siblings have been looked after by them. Although caretaking by older siblings is shown to lack the quality of parental care, both the looked after child and the caretaker can benefit from the occasional experience (Kosonen, 1996).

Worries and fear tend to centre on school and social issues. Concerns about looks, friends, exams and performing in public are common place. Children may also worry about their health, and minor ailments or blemishes are interpreted as a crisis.

The possible impact of parental problems

There are five major issues for this age group: emotional disturbances, conduct disorders including bullying, sexual abuse, the problems of being young carers, and denial of own needs and feelings.

The volatility of this age group means that the impact of parental problems, while similar to that at a younger age group, is more intense. Mothers' mental health problems and in particular depression may result in children showing more behaviour problems than those whose mothers are well (Downey and Coyne, 1990). Other research has suggested that problems can manifest themselves both in terms of emotional disturbances (see for example Lee and Gotlib, 1989) and conduct disorders (see for example Hammen et al, 1978; Beardsley et al, 1987; Klein et al, 1988).

Similarly, research from family violence suggests that children may be deeply affected by events at home. Wolfe et al (1985) found serious behavioural problems were 17 times higher for boys and 10 times higher for girls who witnessed the abuse of their mother. Some children from violent homes may react to frustration with aggression and force. In school this may take the form of bullying, which may be seen by the child as an effective and acceptable way of solving problems.

In addition to findings on bullying there is evidence from clinical studies, of an association between young perpetrators of sexual abuse and childhood experiences of family violence (Monck and New, 1996; Bentovim and Williams, 1998; Skuse et al, 1998). Research by Skuse et al, (1997 and 1998) shows the experience of physical violence, both as victim and as witness, was common among sexually abusing adolescent boys, irrespective of whether or not they had been victims of sexual abuse. But caution must be attached to making simple causal links between being brought up in violent and abusive homes and becoming an abuser (see Morley and Mullender, 1994).

A third major problem for children whose parents are unable to look after them adequately, is that the normal pace of emotional maturity can be accelerated. For some young carers this has resulted in a loss of their childhood. As well as having to take on practical household tasks which are normally carried out by an adult, they have had to assume emotional responsibility for a parent or younger siblings.

> 'Helen (10) described how she had to look after her younger brothers and sisters because "...Mummy's often in bed all morning"' (quoted in ChildLine, 1997, p.24).

Marie (14) describes to ChildLine how she had to look after her mother who was a problem drinker.

> 'I have to tell her when to go to bed, I have to undress her. She is covered in cuts and bruises and never knows where she gets them...She used to be pretty but now she is bloated and lined and looks terrible' (quoted in ChildLine, 1997, p.38).

Conflict between the caring role and the child's own needs can lead to feelings of guilt and resentment (Barnett and Parker, 1998; Edwards and Smith, 1997). Children may be so wrapped up in the needs and feelings of a parent that they find it hard to think or talk about themselves. This preoccupation with their parents can mean that they deny their own needs and feelings (ChildLine, 1997).

Self-care skills

Expected self-care skills

At this age children are becoming increasingly competent. Although they may not always do it willingly, the majority of children of this age are capable of clearing up their own rooms and carrying out simple household tasks. When, for example, shopping for clothes 10 and 11 year olds may still want a parent to accompany them, but by 13 the majority wish to shop with friends.

Children feel confident in staying away from home for short periods and cope adequately with the routines and cultures of other families. They are increasingly able to prepare simple meals, use the telephone with confidence and react appropriately in an emergency.

The possible impact of parental problems

The impact of parental mental illness, problem alcohol or drug use, or domestic violence on young adolescents' self-care skills is that they are forced to assume too much responsibility for themselves and other family members. As a result young carers may fail to look after their own developmental needs.

The experience of being a young carer may mean that children are extremely skilled in carrying out everyday household chores and looking after themselves. However, the feeling of overall responsibility and continual fear of what might happen in their absence, results in some children feeling they must remain continually vigilant. As a result children are absent from home as little as possible and everyday events such as having lunch at school, visiting friends or joining school trips are forgone.

> '...he goes through different stages...I just try to make him feel more comfortable really, because he gets really depressed about things...I just worry when I've got to go to school and that, half the time he's in the house on his own'

(a girl quoted by Edwards and Smith, 1997).

To sum up

Main problems for children aged 10–14 years
- Children have to cope with puberty without support.
- Children are at an increased risk of psychological problems.

- Children fear being hurt.
- Children are at increased risk of actual injury.
- Children are anxious about how to compensate for physical neglect.
- Children's education suffers because they find it difficult concentrate.
- School performance may be below expected ability.
- Children may miss school because of looking after parents or siblings.
- Children reject their families and have low self-esteem.
- Children are cautious of exposing family life to outside scrutiny.
- Friendships are restricted.
- Children fear the family will be broken up.
- Children feel isolated and have no one to turn to.
- Children are at increased risk of emotional disturbance and conduct disorders including bullying.
- An increased risk of sexual abuse in adolescent boys.
- The problems of being a young carer increase.
- Children may be in denial of own needs and feelings.

Protective Factors
- Sufficient income support and good physical standards in the home.
- Practical and domestic help.
- Regular medical and dental checks including school medicals.
- Factual information about puberty, sex and contraception.
- Regular attendance at school.
- Sympathetic, empathic and vigilant teachers.
- Belonging to organised out-of-school activities, including homework clubs.
- A mentor or trusted adult with whom the child is able to discuss sensitive issues.
- An adult who assumes the role of champion, is committed to the child and *'acts vigorously, persistently and painstakingly on their behalf'* (Department of Health, 1996, p.24).
- A mutual friend. Research suggests that positive features in one relationship can compensate for negative qualities in another (Stocker, 1994). Mutual friendship is associated with feelings of self worth (Parker and Asher, 1992 quoted in Stocker, 1994).

- The acquisition of a range of coping strategies and being sufficiently confident to know what to do when parents are incapacitated.

- An ability to separate, either psychologically or physically from the stressful situation.

- Information on how to contact relevant professionals and a contact person in the event of a crisis regarding the parent.

- Unstigmatised support from relevant professionals. Some children derive satisfaction from the caring role and their responsibility for and influence within the family. However, many feel that their role is not sufficiently recognised.

- An alternative, safe and supportive residence for mothers and children subject to violence and the threat of violence.

Children aged 15 and over

Health

Expected health

Taking account of limitations due to disability or an ongoing health condition, there is an expectation that adolescents aged 15 or more can manage their own health needs. Adolescents should certainly be able to seek advice from parents, carers or doctors.

Many teenage girls dislike the changes puberty brings to the shape of their bodies and strive to retain or regain their childlike figures '...*by late teens and early twenties, up to half of girls have dieted, usually without success*' (Leffert and Petersen, 1995, p.69).

There is an increasing experimentation with drugs and alcohol. Some 70% of young people in England have tried smoking, and over a quarter (28%) smoke on a regular basis (O.P.C.S. 1995). A third of 15–year-old boys claim to drink regularly and 28% of same aged girls. Afro-Caribbean and White children were found most likely to have tried alcohol, 71% and 65% respectively compared with only 19% of Asian children (Health Education Authority, 1992).

Illicit drug use also increases. One study suggests that 45% of young people aged 16–19 will have taken one or more drugs at some time in their lives, although regular consumption is less usual (15% took drugs in the past month). Drug use is associated with social class. The higher the social class the more likely the young person will have experimented with illicit drugs (Leitner, 1993). The most widely used drug is cannabis followed by various 'hallucinates' including amphetamines, LSD, 'magic mushrooms' and ecstasy. The consumption of heroin and crack or methadone and cocaine is extremely rare (Ramsey and Spiller, 1997).

Late adolescence is also a period of sexual experimentation, it is a time when many young people embark on their first sexual relationship (see Department of Health, 1996).

The possible impact of parental problems

There are three main health issues for teenagers: inappropriate role models, greater risk of accidents, and problems related to sexual relationships.

There is considerable evidence that problem alcohol or drug use by parents is associated with alcohol and drug use by the children (see Hogan, 1998; Velleman, 1993). What is less clear is the relative role and significance of genetic and environmental factors. For example genetics may play a role in determining levels of consumption and metabolism of alcohol.

It is generally accepted that alcohol and drug use is the result of a combination of many factors such as culture, childhood experiences and social circumstances. Recent research has identified three issues which are significant predictors of young people's vulnerability to tobacco, alcohol and cannabis use: the affiliation with a delinquent or drug using sub-culture, the wish for novelty, and parental illicit drug use (Lynskey et al, 1989). The picure is further complicated because parental attitudes may be more relevant to the adolescent's drug use than actual parental behaviour. Indeed, the relationship between extreme parental attitudes and behaviours and children's reactions may be complex. As noted earlier, children may adopt equally extreme but opposite positions (Orford and Velleman, 1990; Velleman, 1993).

Excessive parental drinking may have an indirect impact on young people's health if it results in young people mirroring their behaviour. Research has shown that children who start drinking at an early age are at greater risk of being involved in accidents; drinking is a contributory factor in 20 to 30 per cent of all accidents. *'Young, inexperienced drivers are over-represented in deaths from drink-driving; nearly a third of pedestrians killed aged 16 to 19 had been drinking'* (Walker, 1995).

Adolescents, whose parents are absorbed in their own problems and are emotionally unavailable and insensitive to their children's needs, may be at increased risk of pregnancy or getting someone pregnant, or catching a sexually transmitted disease. Not being physically or emotionally available can mean children have not had the opportunity to discuss contraception or, equally important, how to develop strategies to act effectively in close personal relationships. Similarly, young people need a degree of self-confidence to be able to influence what happens to them in a sexual relationship (Department of Health, 1996). Growing up in a situation of domestic violence or with parents with alcohol or drug problems, has a negative impact on young people's self-confidence.

Education and cognitive ability

Expected education

The majority (71.5%) of children aged 16 years are in full-time education and a further 17% attend some form of training (Department for Education and Employment, 1996). Most young people in compulsory education attend school regularly. Only *'6% of 5th form pupils were serious truants'* (Gray and Jesson, 1989 cited in Carlen et al, 1992). Young people need guidance to ensure their education is properly planned and suits their ambitions and abilities.

Examinations can cause many teenagers, particularly those who are prone to anxiety, considerable stress. Although the majority cope, a mentor in the form of a parent or teacher who offers support both academic and emotional, can obviate negative outcomes (Hodge et al, 1997).

The possible impact of parental problems

There are several areas where parental problems can impact upon children's performance at school: a failure to achieve potential; behaviour which leads to school exclusion; and a lack of attainment which may affect long-term life chances.

The first problem facing teenagers' educational progress is that the stresses of coping with parental problems and undertaking the care of younger siblings can take its toll on their education.

> *'Homework being handed in late, being very tired, once I fell asleep at school and being absent'*, was how a 15 year old girl summed it up (Brisby et al, 1997).

When education is interrupted and teenagers fail to reach their potential this can have long-term negative consequences for their future employment prospects. Research has shown that qualifications earned at the age of 16 are the best single predictor of the direction an individual's career will take (Banks et al, 1992).

Secondly, there is evidence for an association between mental health problems in parents and children's academic attainment. For example, Weissman et al (1984) and Downey et al (1990) found a significant association between maternal depression and academic failures and school based problems. However, Emery et al (1982) failed to find the link for depression but showed an association between parents diagnosed with schizophrenia and higher incidence of school behaviour problems in teenagers.

If disturbed behaviour results in exclusion from school, teenagers need an adult to champion their cause, strive for their re-entry or ensure their learning continues (Department of Health, 1996). This is important not only because school qualifications are strong predictors of future careers (Banks et al, 1992), but also because many excluded pupils have few if any friends (Galloway et al, 1982). However, parental problems may leave teenagers without a champion.

Finally, a lack of educational attainment has long-term effects on children's life chances. A large body of research suggests that early school leavers who are unemployed have much poorer mental health than those who have a job (see for example Stafford et al, 1980; Donovan and Oddy, 1982; Warr et al, 1985). Practically half of all 16 year olds who do not continue their education are unemployed (Department for Education and Employment, 1997).

Identity

Expected identity

Fifteen-year-olds experience a growing self-awareness and struggle to sort out their own potential and limitations. Their sense of identity is made up of a combination of 'given' elements, an understanding and interpretation of past events, and the impact of present incidents and expectations for the future. Many teenagers experiment with a range of different identities, some of which may come into conflict with parental expectations.

The young person's sense of identity is linked to a feeling of belonging to their family. Even when teenagers reject family values and culture, long lasting rifts are unusual (Rutter et al, 1976). Although teenagers become more peer oriented, parents still have considerable influence on specific areas of life such as educational plans and future life goals. Peers, on the other hand, exert more influence on every day issues such as choice of clothes, use of leisure time, drinking and drug use (Smith and Cowie, 1991).

The possible impact of parental problems

There are two main issues which present themselves in relation to the impact of parental mental illness, problem alcohol or drug use, or domestic violence on young people's sense of identity: low self-esteem and the consequences of inconsistent parenting.

Some teenagers of parents who have alcohol problems have low self-esteem and fear that they will turn out like their parents.

> *'I've been involved with drinking, drugs, fighting, I'm desperate to change. I don't want to be like Dad'* (Roy (16) talking to ChildLine, 1997, p.33).

When young people have grown up in families where little is predictable or reliable, they are likely to believe that they have little control over what happens to them (ChildLine, 1997).

Family and social relationships

Expected relationship

Parent-adolescent relationships remain strong although they undergo considerable change as the child increasingly strives for more autonomy and parents demand greater levels of responsible behaviour. There is a gradual shift from parent regulated behaviour to co-regulation and autonomous functioning (Leffert and Petersen, 1995). Nonetheless, adolescents wish for harmonious relationships with parents and these remain an important source of emotional support (Hartup, 1983).

Friends become increasingly important and influential in the lives of young people. Relationships with friends differ in quality from those of middle childhood. Adolescent friendships tend to be more intimate and involve more mutual exchanges of thoughts and feelings, and shared activities (Hartup, 1983). Single sex peer groups are on the decline.

Most adolescents are striving to become confident in their sexual orientation. It is the age when many young people fall in love and embark on their first sexual encounter. The median age of reported first sexual intercourse by women aged 16 to 24 years is 17 years (Leffert and Petersen, 1995). The first love affair constitutes a most important emotional experience for teenagers and its break-up engenders considerable stress.

The possible impact of parental problems

There are three issues with regard to the impact of parental mental illness, problem alcohol or drug use, or domestic violence and young people's relationships. First, the problem reported by adolescents is their feeling of isolation from both friends and adults outside the family. Second, the wish to escape can place young people in very vulnerable positions. Third, the experience of domestic violence effects young people's own dating behaviour.

Adolescents may feel isolated because they wish to keep adult and peer friends separate from family difficulties; alternatively they may not wish to burden friends with their problems (Brisby et al, 1997).

Fourteen year old Louise's isolation is all too evident. She rang ChildLine to say that her mother was threatening to leave her father because of his drink problem.

> 'Her mother said she wanted to take them but couldn't. "I feel very sad all the time...I feel like running away...I have no-one I can talk to" (ChildLine, 1997, p.25).

The consequence of this isolation is that adolescents frequently cope with family stress, arguments and violence by escaping. Adolescents may escape by withdrawing into themselves, characterised by long periods of day-dreaming, or time spent in their bed room or out of the house.

A more risky method of escape is to run away. The most common reason young people run away from home is a background of neglect associated with parental problem drinking or drug use (Wade and Biehal, 1998). A higher incidence of running away from home and youth homelessness was found amongst children from families where there was domestic violence. Hester and Radford (1996) indicate a quarter (26%) of homeless 16–25 year olds left home due to domestic violence.

Alternatively, young people may seek escape and solace in drugs and alcohol. To enable young people to find less damaging ways of coping with family stress depends on a caring person establishing a relationship characterised by mutual trust and respect. Unfortunately, many young people growing up in very dysfunctional families have learnt to distrust adults (Department of Health, 1996).

Research suggests that witnessing the abuse of their mothers is associated with teenage boys taking an aggressive, angry and abusing role during dates. Dating violence among young males is linked to a childhood experience of domestic violence (Moffitt, 1993).

Social presentation

Expected presentation

Young people are able to take care of themselves. They can take control for their own clothes, hair and skin care. They can choose the appropriate clothing to suit different occasions and rarely take advice on what to wear. Young people's appearance continues to be an extremely important issue. A considerable proportion of many young people's disposable income is spent on clothing and toiletries.

Young people are increasingly competent in adjusting their behaviour, conversation and dress to different situations.

The possible impact of parental problems

The problems for social presentation are a lack of guidance to moderate the extremes of dress and presentation, insufficient funds for adequate or appropriate clothing and toiletries, and the use of aggression inappropriately to solve problems.

When adolescents feel rejected or alienated from their families they may resort to extreme modes of dress, body mutilation or adornment in a gesture of independence. When parents are over-whelmed with their own problems they may not be able to offer the necessary reassurance or guidance to moderate adolescent extremes.

When money and household resources are used to satisfy parental needs for alcohol or illicit drugs, the remaining funds may be insufficient to ensure adolescents can 'keep up appearances'. Because appearance is a priority for adolescents, those with little parental guidance may avoid peer ridicule by resorting to stealing what they want.

To have grown up in a culture of family violence may result in young people resorting to aggression as a method of solving their own problems. Adolescents who cannot control their emotions and react aggressively to peers or adults not only jeopardise their friendships but place their school or work careers at risk through exclusion or encounters with the law.

Emotional and behavioural development

Expected development

The considerable physical and emotional changes which teenagers are undergoing render them vulnerable. It is however, reassuring that rates of severely disturbed behaviour among this age group continue to be relatively low. Only 13.2% of boys and 12.5% of girls aged 14–15 years were found to have a psychiatric disorder (Rutter et al, 1976). By contrast, there is a considerable body of research which indicates depressive feelings and depressive disorders increase during adolescence (see Fombonne, 1995 for an overview of this research). It is worthy of note, that in adolescents, depressive disorders are twice as high among girls as among boys.

Suicide, like depressive disorders, is also more common during adolescence. The most rapid rise is between the ages of 15 and 19 years. Gender also appears to influence the outcome of suicide attempts. Boys outnumber girls in completed suicides, while girls outnumber boys in suicidal behaviour (Fombonne, 1995).

The possible impact of parental problems

There are three major areas that affect teenagers' emotional and behavioural development: the emotional problems that result from self-blame and guilt, possible increased risk of suicidal behaviour, and vulnerability to conduct disorders and crime.

The first problem is that the tendency to blame themselves, an issue already discussed in relation to younger children, continues through late adolescence. Teenagers continue to feel responsible for their parents' behaviour and believe they are unloved and unlovable.

Cindy (15) told ChildLine *'Dad drinks and hits Mum. I took an overdose last week – I want to die. I can't talk to Mum because it would only add to her problems. It's all my fault'* (ChildLine, 1997, p.26).

The tendency for suicidal behaviour to increase in adolescence has already been discussed. There remains the exploration of any association between parents' problems and an increased risk of suicidal behaviour and depression. Although earlier research has suggested that teenage children of depressives are at increased risk of suicidal behaviour and depression (Weissman et al, 1986) more recent research offers little substantiation. Diekstra et al's (1995) review of research findings concluded that suicidal behaviour in adolescents is associated with a history of physical and sexual abuse. However, no such associative link was found for adolescent suicidal behaviour and parental depression, personality or psychotic disorders.

Adolescents may also be at risk because they resort to illegitimate methods of acquiring funds when everyday household monies are spent on gratifying parental drinking or drug needs. Alternatively they may come in contact with the law because of their anti-social behaviour. Recent research suggests anti-social and delinquent behaviours peak during late adolescence, and children of parents who are problem drug users are particularly at risk (Moffitt, 1993).

Self-care skills

Expected self-care skills

By 15 and 16 years most young people are capable of looking after their own basic needs. For example, they can wash up, shop, cook a simple meal and look after their clothes. The majority will know how to use public transport and can organise their own travel arrangements.

Young people should be able to function independently at a level appropriate to their age and cognitive and physical ability. But, however well they appear to cope, young people need an adult to whom they can turn to for help and advice when necessary.

The possible impact of parental problems

As we have already noted for children aged 10–14 years, being a young carer results in practical skills well beyond their years. As adulthood approaches many adolescents continue to feel responsible for their parents and younger siblings. When away from home many continue to worry about their parents' welfare or that of younger siblings. This may result in young people leading a restricted life.

> 'My mum was depressed, I was unable to be with my friends...I looked after her all the time, I did the cleaning, the tidying, the washing up and the shopping. If I was out I was worried about her and I would come rushing back' (NSPCC, 1997a, p.38).

To sum up

Main problems for children aged 15 years and over

- Teenagers have inappropriate role models.

- Teenagers are at greater risk of accidents.

- Teenagers may have problems related to sexual relationships.

- Teenagers may fail to achieve their potential.

- Teenagers are at increased risk of school exclusion.

- Poor life chances due to exclusion and poor school attainment.

- Low self-esteem as a consequence of inconsistent parenting.

- Increased isolation from both friends and adults outside the family.

- Teenagers may use aggression inappropriately to solve problems.

- Emotional problems may result from self-blame and guilt, and lead to increased risk of suicidal behaviour, and vulnerability to crime.

- Teenagers' own needs may be sacrificed to meet the needs of their parents.

Protective factors

- Sufficient income support and good physical standards in the home.

- Practical and domestic help.

- Regular medical and dental checks.

- Factual information about sex and contraception.

- Regular attendance at school or a form of further education.

- Sympathetic, empathic and vigilant teachers.

- For those who are no longer in full time education, a job.

- A trusted adult with whom the young person is able to discuss sensitive issues.

- An adult who acts as a champion, is committed to the young person and *'acts vigorously, persistently and painstakingly on their behalf'* (Department of Health, 1996, p.24).

- A mutual friend. Research suggests that positive features in one relationship can compensate for negative qualities in another (Stocker, 1994). Mutual friendship is associated with feelings of self-worth (Parker and Asher, 1992 quoted in Stocker, 1994).

- The acquisition of a range of coping strategies and being sufficiently confident to know what to do when parents are incapacitated.

- An ability to separate, either psychologically or physically, from the stressful situation.

- Information on how to contact relevant professionals and a contact person in the event of a crisis regarding the parent.

- When young people act as carers, and experience a degree of satisfaction and control this may act as a protective factor (NSPCC, 1997a).

- Unstigmatised support from relevant professionals who recognise their role as a young carer.

- An alternative, safe and supportive residence for young people subject to violence and the threat of violence.

Conclusion

This detailed exploration of the impact of parental mental illness, problem drinking or drug use, or domestic violence on children's health and development at different stages of life highlights the importance of looking at children and families as individuals. The short and long-term consequences for children of growing up in a family where at least one parent is experiencing extreme difficulties will depend on the combination of resilience and protective mechanisms. For example, when parental mental illness or problem drinking is accompanied by domestic violence or associated with poverty and social isolation, children are particularly vulnerable. However, other factors, such as the availability of other caring adults, may cushion the negative consequences. It is therefore important not to pathologise all children who live in families where a parent suffers from mental illness, problem drinking or drug use, or domestic violence. The challenge to practitioners is to identify:

- Which children need help and the level of concern

- Which aspects of development are being adversely affected and how

- What services are needed to help both the child and the family.

Part five:

Implications for policy and practice

Comprehensive assessment and intervention

- Mental illness, problem alcohol and drug use, or domestic violence affect people in their parenting ability and impact on their children in variable ways. Therefore, skilled, comprehensive and holistic assessments which place equal emphasis on the child, family and environment, are essential.

- Services to the family can be provided under children's or adult legislation. This can have positive benefits or result in children falling between the two stools of different service areas. To ensure integrated service provision, specific attention must be given to creating professional links between community care and children's services.

- The varying effects of parental mental illness, problem drinking and drug use, or domestic violence demands careful assessment of children's needs. For example, some children may take on caring responsibilities within the family as a result. Too often little attention is paid to this issue.

- Young carers may be defined as children in need. This allows services, such as befriending, counselling, respite care and recreational facilities to be provided. Thus, in line with Department of Health Guidance, service intervention should be designed to support children and young people and to minimise the burden and negative effects of being a young carer in these circumstances.

- Many of these families fear that revealing their problems will lead to punitive reactions by service providers. Access to services needs to be non-stigmatising.

- Interventions which reduce the stress mothers' experience is likely to benefit children indirectly. 'Community mothers', voluntary befriending schemes and other social support interventions for mothers of young children, for example HomeStart and Newpin, can provide essential help. Such programmes should be expanded and funded by adult and children's services, and by health as well as social services.

- The key worker system is another important intervention strategy. The key worker is the point of contact for the family and coordinator of services. Key workers in these situations should be experienced in both child care and adult services and should have sufficient professional authority for all other professionals to feel able to delegate responsibility to them. They should be able to act both as a case manager and carry out direct work with children and carers. The key worker acts not only as a pivot for the family but also as a link between the different agencies involved. This is essential since a multi-agency approach is critical in order to ensure children's educational and health needs are fully met.

- A further important aspect of the intervention is specifically directed work with children. Children's needs will vary. While some children cope well, others will benefit from advice, assistance and counselling. For a minority, intensive therapeutic intervention will be needed to overcome the traumatic effect of parental problems.

Joint working

- Since parents frequently experience more than one of the three problems: mental illness, problem drinking or drug use, or domestic violence communication, co-ordination and collaboration between a wide range of agencies is an imperative.

- Collaboration across organisational and agency boundaries should be established to ensure co-ordinated assessment, care planning and service delivery by adult and children's teams for individual families. Specific forums or working groups may be required.

- Professionals tend to focus on the needs of their specific client group. When the needs of their client are at odds with the needs of others in the family they may feel the need to advocate on their behalf. This may result in polarised views which block effective joint working. There is a need for balanced considerations across all services and due consideration given to the needs of all family members. General knowledge of the issues among all professionals needs to be increased.

- An organisational barrier to working together is the different notions of confidentiality held by different professionals and agencies. Strategies for communicating about the families across agency lines need to be developed and if necessary protocols agreed on similar lines to those in child protection. For example, Birmingham Social Services and the West Midlands Police have developed an integrated approach to domestic violence and child protection.

- Although social services departments have a key role to play, not all children and young carers are in contact with social services. Identifying young carers is most likely to fall to other professionals: the family doctor, community or district nurses and health visitors. Alternatively, children may reveal their problems at school. Thus, strategies for encouraging referrals from alternative sources are needed for families and children to be well served.

- Joint commissioning and joint planning groups are likely to play an important role. *'In particular, the Children's Services Plan and the Community Care Plan can and should address these needs and commissioners should ensure that contract specifications encourage providers to collaborate'* (Brisby et al, 1997, p.25).

Flexible time frames

- Some family needs may be long-term. 'Multi-problem' families experience problems which cross-agency boundaries and are likely to continue for some considerable time. Short-term interventions for these families are rarely effective. In 'acutely distressed' families, where parental problems have overwhelmed family resources, short-term interventions have been shown to be very effective (Cleaver and Freeman, 1995).

- Agencies need to develop operational policies appropriate to the needs of different families over time. In some cases, there is likely to be continuous action by one or more agency. To prevent families drifting clear objectives need to be set. Once cases have been allocated, continuous monitoring, reviewing and planning and clear allocation of responsibilities and accountability between agencies will be needed. The continuity of a worker will be of considerable value. Other cases may be closed because families are able to cope. However, crises may continue to occur and families need to know that they can come back, ask for help at any time, be welcomed and have easy access to services. This also requires operational case policies to be developed.

- By contrast in 'single issue' families where there may be no other problems except for the presenting one, for example, the mental illness or problem drinking suffered by one parent, the strengths and supports in the family may ensure that few aspects of children's development and welfare are at risk of suffering significant harm. In these cases the input of a single agency may be all that is needed. Nonetheless, the active agency should still be alert to the needs of all the family.

- The needs of every family should be considered individually and the appropriate time frame for services established accordingly.

Information for children and families

- Families and especially children and young carers need sensitively developed information telling them about the problems they are experiencing and their implications.

- Families also need information about the range of services available in their local community, including how the interface between adult and children's services is bridged.

- Knowing what to expect when approaching agencies for help can be very reassuring to families. Families need information on how to gain access to services and what to expect when entering service systems.

- The information needs to be widely available, written in relevant languages, and produced in an accessible format. Additional consideration should be given to ensuring information is produced in a form accessible to those with communication difficulties (both adults and children).

- These families are likely to have specialised needs for information. For example, children who become young carers need an identified person as an 'anchor' who they can easily contact in times of crisis or for information when worried.

Training and educational needs

- In order to achieve effectively co-ordinated services, training must be provided on a multi disciplinary and cross-agency basis.

- The general public need to be better educated on the issues for families experiencing parental mental illness, alcohol or drug problems, or domestic violence. The aim would be to ensure that these families can be better supported with a higher level of understanding in their communities and by their extended family networks.

- Professional training programmes need to incorporate more information on the effects of parental mental illness, alcohol and drug problems, or domestic violence, on both parents and their children. Training should draw on evidence from research.

- Joint training between adult and children's services staff and other agencies is needed to ensure that different professionals develop and use a common language. Training will need to ensure that issues of race, culture and disability are taken into account so that sensitive practice is developed.

- Professionals who work primarily with children need training to recognise and identify parents' problems and the effects these may have on children. Alternatively, training for professionals working with adults needs to cover the impact parental problems may have on children. For example, *'Police training must be improved so that all police officers, not just those in specialist units, have a better understanding of the impact of domestic violence on children'* (NCH, 1994 p.23).

- Training is needed to ensure that staff in agencies dealing with adults have the necessary skills in communicating with children.

- Training and guidance to the judiciary needs to improve so that the effect of domestic violence on children is better understood and violence against women and children is treated seriously in all jurisdictions.

Bibliography

Abel, E.L. (1997) 'Maternal alcohol consumption and spontaneous abortion', *Alcohol and Alcoholism*, Vol.32, No.3, pp.211–219.

Abel, E.L. and Sokol, R. (1991) 'A revised conservative estimate of the incidence of foetal alcohol syndrome and its economic impact', *Alcoholism: Clinical and Experimental Research*, Vol.15, pp.514–524.

Ainsworth, M.D.S., Blehar, M.C., Waters, E. and Wall, S. (1978) *Patterns of Attachment: A Psychological Study of the Strange Situation*, Hillsdale, NJ: Erlbaum.

Aldgate, J. (1991) 'Attachment theory and its application to child care social work – an introduction,' in Lishman, J., (ed) *Handbook of Theory for Practice Teachers in Social Work*, London: Jessica Kingsley.

Aldgate, J. and Bradley, M. (in press) *Supporting Families through Short Term Fostering*, London: The Stationery Office.

Aldgate, J. and Tunstill, J. (1995) *Making Sense of Section 17*, London, HMSO.

Aldridge J. and Becker, S. (1993) *Children Who Care: Inside the World of Young Carers*, Department of Social Sciences: Loughborough University.

Amato, P.R. (1991) 'Parental absence during childhood and depression in later life', *Sociological Quarterly*, Vol.32, No.4, pp.543–556.

American Psychiatric Association (1994) *Diagnostic and Statistical Manual of Mental Disorders, Fourth Edition (DSM-IV)*, Washington DC: American Psychiatric Association.

Andrews, B. and Brown, G.W. (1988) 'Marital violence in the community: a biographical approach', *British Journal of Psychiatry*, Vol.153, pp.305–312.

Anthony, E.J. (1974) 'The syndrome of the psychologically invulnerable child', in: Anthony, E.J. and Koupernik (eds) *The Child and His Family: Children at Psychiatric Risk*, 3. New York: Wiley.

Avis, H. (1993) *Drugs and Life*, 2nd edition, Brown and Benchmark.

Baker, O. and Marsden, J. (1994) *Drug Misuse in Britain*, London: ISDD.

Bamrah, J.S., Freeman, H.L. and Goldber, D.P. (1991) 'Epidemiology of schizophrenia in Salford, 1974–84,' *British Journal of Psychiatry*, Vol.159, pp.802–810.

Banks, M., Bates, I., Breakwell, G., Bynner, J., Emler, W., Jamieson, L. and Roberts, K. (1992) *Careers and Identities*, Buckingham: Open University Press.

Barnett, B, & Parker, G. (1998) 'The parentified child: Early competence or childhood deprivation', *Child Psychology & Psychiatry, Review*, Vol.3, No.4. pp.146–155.

Beardsley, W.R., Schultz, L.H. and Selman, R.L. (1987) 'Level of social cognitive development, adaptive functioning and DSM-111 diagnoses in adolescent offspring of parents with affective disorder: Implications of the development of capacity for mutuality', *Developmental Psychology*, Vol.23, pp.807–815.

Bebbington, A. and Miles, J. (1989) 'The background of children who enter local authority care', *British Journal of Social Work*, Vol.19, pp.349–368.

Bentovim, A. and Williams, B. (1998) 'Children and adolescents: victims who become perpetrators', *Advances in Psychiatric Treatment*, Vol.4, pp.101–107.

Bettes, B.A. (1988) 'Maternal depression and motherese: Temporal and interactional features', *Child Development*, Vol.59, pp.1089–1096.

Billings, A.G. et al (1979) 'Marital conflict resolution of alcoholic and non alcoholic couples during drinking and nondrinking sessions', *Journal of Studies on Alcohol*, Vol. 40, No.3, pp.183–195.

Billings, A.G. and Moos, R.H. (1985) 'Children of parents with unipolar depression: a controlled one year follow-up', *Journal of Abnormal Child Psychology*, Vol.14, pp.149–166.

Birtchnell, J. and Kennard, J. (1983) 'Marriage and mental illness', *British Journal of Psychiatry*, Vol.142, pp.193–198.

Blane, H.T. (1988) 'Prevention issues with children of alcoholics', *British Journal of Addiction*, Vol.83, No.7, pp.793–798.

Bowker, L.H., Arbitell, M. and McFerron, J.R. (1988) 'On the relationship between wife beating and child abuse', in Yllo, K. and

Bograd, M. (eds.) *Feminist Perspectives on Wife Abuse,* Newbury Park, California: Sage.

Bowlby, J. (1969) *Attachment and Loss,* Volume 1, London: Hogarth Press.

Bradshaw, J. (1990) *Child Poverty and Deprivation in the U.K.,* London: N.C.B.

Brandon, M.M. and Lewis, A. (1996) 'Significant harm and children's experiences of domestic violence', *Child and Family Social Work,* Vol.1, No.1, pp.33–42.

Breznitz, Z. and Friedman, S.L. (1988) 'Toddlers' concentration: does maternal depression make a difference', *Journal of Child Psychology and Psychiatry and Allied Disciplines,* Vol.29, No.3, pp.267–279.

Brisby, T., Baker, S. and Hedderwick, T. (1997) *Under the Influence: Coping with parents who drink too much,* London: Alcohol Concern.

British Crime Survey (1996) London: Home Office.

Brown, G.W. and Harris, T. (1978) *Social Origins of Depression,* Tavistock: London.

Browne, K. and Saqi, S. (1987) Parent-child interactions in abusing families and its possible causes and consequences, in Maher, P. (ed.) *Child Abuse: The Educational Perspective,* Oxford, Blackwell.

Burns, E.C. (1996) 'The health and development of children whose mothers are on methadone maintenance', *Child Abuse Review,* Vol.5, pp.113–122.

Burstein, I., Kinch, R.A.H. and Stern, L. (1974) 'Anxiety, pregnancy, labor and the neonate', *Am. J. Obstet. Gynec.,* Vol.118, pp.195–199.

Caplan, H.L., Cogill, S.R., Alexandra, H. and Robinson, K.M. (1989) 'Maternal depression and the emotional development of the child', *British Journal of Psychiatry,* Vol.154, pp.818–822.

Carlen, P., Gleeson, D. and Wardhaugh, J. (1992) *Truancy: The Politics of Compulsory Schooling,* Buckingham, Open University Press.

Carroll, J. (1994) 'The protection of children exposed to marital violence', *Child Abuse Review,* Vol.3, pp.6–14.

Casey, M. (1987) *Domestic Violence Against Women,* Dublin: Dublin Federation of Refuges.

Cassin, A.L. (1996) 'Acute maternal mental illness – infants at risk: A community focus', *Psychiatric Care*, Vol.2, No.6, pp.202–205.

Casswell, S. (1991) 'A longitudinal study of New Zealand children's experience with alcohol', *British Journal of Addiction*, Vol.86, No.3, pp.277–85.

Cazdin, A.E. (1990) 'Psychotherapy for Children and Adolescents', *Annual Review of Psychology*, Vol.41, pp.21–54.

ChildLine, (1997) *Beyond the limit: children who live with parental alcohol misuse*, London: ChildLine.

Children Act 1948 (11 and 120 Geo.6, C.43).

Cleaver, H. and Freeman, P. (1995) *Parental Perspectives in Cases of Suspected Child Abuse*, London: HMSO.

Cicchetti, D., and Toth, S.L. (1995) 'A developmental psychopathology perspective on child abuse and neglect', *J. Am. Acad. Child Adolesc. Psychiatry*, Vol.34, No.5, pp.541–565.

Cleaver, H. and Freeman, P. (1996) 'Child abuse which involves wider kin and family friends', in Bibby, P. (ed.) *Organised Abuse: The Current Debate*, London: Arena.

Cohler, B., Grunebaum, H., Weiss, J., Gamer, E. and Gallant, D. (1977) 'Disturbance of attention among schizophrenic, depressed, and well mothers and their young children', *Journal of Child Psychology and Psychiatry*, Vol.18, pp.115–164.

Coleman, R. and Cassell, D. (1995) 'Parents who misuse drugs and alcohol', in Reder P. and Lucey, C. (eds.) *Assessment of Parenting: Psychiatric and Psychological Contributions*, London: Routledge.

Colton, M.E. (1980) quoted in Hogan, D.M. (1998) 'The psychological development and welfare of children of opiate and cocaine users: review and research needs', *Journal of Child Psychology and Psychiatry*, Vol.39, No.5, pp.609–620.

Cook, P.W. (1997) *Abused Men: the hidden side of domestic violence*, Westport, Praeger.

Cooper, P.J., Campbell, E.A., Day, A. et al., (1988) 'Non-psychotic psychiatric disorder after childbirth: A prospective study of prevalence, incidence, course and natures', *British Journal of Psychiatry*, Vol.152, pp.799–806.

Cork, R,M. (1969) *The Forgotten Children: A Study of Children of Alcoholic Parents*, Toronto: Paper Jacks.

Corob, A. (1987) *Working with depressed women: a feminist approach*, Aldershot: Gower.

Coulter, J. (1973) *Approaches to Insantity: A Philosphical and Sociological Study*, London, Robertson.

Courtney, M.E., Barth, R.P., Berrick, J.D., Brooks, D., Needell, B. and Park, L. (1996) 'Race and Child Welfare Services: Past Research and Future Directions', *Child Welfare League of America*, Vol.LXXV, No.2, pp.99–137.

Cox, A.D., Puckering, C., Pound, A and Mills, M. (1987) 'The impact of maternal depression in young children', *Journal of Child Psychology and Psychiatry*, Vol.28, pp.917–928.

Cummings, E.M. and Davies, P.T. (1994) 'Maternal depression and child development', *Journal of Child Psychology and Psychiatry*, Vol.35, No.1, pp.73–112.

Davenport, Y.B. Zahn-Waxler, C., Adland, M.C. and Mayfiled, A. (1984) 'Early child-rearing practices in families with a manic-depressive parent', *American Journal of Psychiatry* , Vol.141, pp.230–235.

Dawe, S., Gerada, J. and Strang, J. (1992) 'Establishment of a liaison service for pregnant opiate dependent women', *British Journal of Addictions*, Vol.87, No.6, pp.867–871.

Deane, S. (1996) *Reading in the Dark,* London,Vintage.

Dearden, C. and Becker, S. (1995) *Young Carers: The Facts*, London: Community Care.

d'Orban, P.T. (1979) 'Women who kill their children', *British Journal of Psychiatry*, Vol.134, pp.560–571.

Department for Education and Employment (1996) *Education facts and figures England 1996*, Darlington: Department for Education and Employment.

Department for Education and Employment (1997) *School Leavers Destinations Surveys: Careers Service Activity Survey,* Darlington: Department for Education and Employment.

Department of Health (1990) *The National Health Service and Community Care Act 1990*, London: HMSO.

Department of Health (1991) *The Care of Children: Principles and Practice in Guidance and Regulations*, London: HMSO.

Department of Health (1995a) *Child Protection: Messages from Research*, London: HMSO.

Department of Health (1995b) *Looking After Children: Assessment and Action Reconds, Age Three and Four Years*, London: HMSO.

Department of Health (1996) *Focus on Teenagers: Research into Practice*, London: HMSO.

Department of Health (1997a) *Children's Services News*, 10.

Department of Health (1997b) *Local Authority Circular LAC(97)15 Family Law Act 1996 Part 1V Family Homes and Domestic Violence*, London: Department of Health.

Department of Health (1997c) *Young Carers: Making a Start*, London: Department of Health.

Department of Health (1998) *Modernising Social Services*, Cm4169, Stationery Office.

Diekstra, R.F.W., Kienhorst, C.W.M. and de Wilde, E.J. (1995) 'Suicide and suicidal behaviour among adolescents', in Rutter, M. and Smith D. (eds) *Psychosocial Disorders in Young People: Time Trends and Their Causes*, Chichester: Wiley.

Dobash, R. E. and Dobash, R.P. (1980) *Violence against Wives*, Sussex: Open Books.

Dobash, R. E. and Dobash, R.P. (1984) 'The nature and antecedents of violent events', *British Journal of Criminology*, Vol.24, No.3, pp.269–288.

Dobash, R. E. and Dobash, R.P. (1992) *Women, Violence and Social Change*, London: Routledge.

Dominy, N. and Radford, L. (1996) *Domestic Violence in Surrey: Towards an Effective Inter-Agency Response*, London Rochampton Institutes/Surrey Social Services.

Donovan, A. and Oddy, M. (1982) 'Psychological aspects of unemployment: An investigation into the emotional and social adjustment of school leavers', *Journal of Adolescence*, Vol.5, pp.15–30.

Dore, M.M. and Dore, J.M. (1995) 'Identifying substance abuse in maltreating families: a child welfare challenge', *Child Abuse and Neglect,* Vol.19, No.5, pp.531–543.

Downey, G. and Coyne J.C. (1990) 'Children of depressed parents: an integrative review', *Psychological Bulletin,* Vol.1, pp.50–76.

Doyle, R. (1994) *Paddy Clarke Ha Ha Ha,* Berkshire: Minerva.

Dunn, J. and McGuire, S. (1992) 'Sibling and Peer Relationships in Childhood', *Journal of Child Psycholology and Psychiatry,* Vol.33, No.1, pp.67–105.

Edwards, A and Smith, P. (1997) 'Young carers and their parents with long term psychiatric disorders', *Keeping Children in Mind: Balancing Children's Needs with Parents' Mental Health,* Report of the 12th Annual Conference hosted by the Michael Sieff Foundation.

Eekelaar, J. and Clive, E. (1977) *Custody after Divorce,* Oxford: Oxford Centre for Socio-Legal Studies, Wolfson College.

Egeland, B. and Scroufe, L.A. (1981) 'Developmental sequelae of maltreatment in infancy', *New Directions in Child Development,* Vol.11, pp.77–92.

Emery, R.E. (1982) 'Interparental conflict and the children of discord and divorce', *Psychological Bulletin,* Vol.92, pp.310–330.

Emery, R., Weintraub, S. and Neale, J.M. (1982) 'Effects of marital discord on the school behavior of children of schizophrenic, affectively disordered, and normal parents,' *Journal of Abnormal Child Psychology,* Vol.10, No.2, pp.215–228.

European Collaborative Study (1991) 'Children born to women with HIV-1 infection: Natural histroy and risk of transmission', *Lancet,* Vol.337, pp.253–258.

Falhberg, V.I. (1991) *A Child's Journey through Placement,* BAAF: London.

Falkov, A. (1996) *A Study of Working Together "Part 8" Reports: Fatal child abuse and parental psychiatric disorder,* DOH-ACPC Series, I, London.

Falkov, A, (1997) 'Adult psychiatry – A missing link in the child protection network: A response to Reder and Duncan', *Child Abuse Review,* Vol.6, pp.41–45.

Falkov, A (forthcoming) *Crossing Bridges*, a draft report to the Department of Health.

Famularo, R., Kinscherff, R. and Fenton, T. (1992) 'Parental substance abuse and the nature of child maltreatment', *Child Abuse and Neglect,* Vol.16, pp. 475–483.

Fantuzzo, J.W. and Lindquist, C.U. (1989) 'The effects of observing conjugal violence on children: a review and analysis of research methodology', *Journal of Family Violence,* Vol.4, No.1, pp.77–94.

Farmer, E. and Owen, (1995) *Child Protection Practice: Private Risks and Public Remedies,* London, HMSO.

Feldman, R.A., Stiffman, A.R. and Jung, K.G. (1987) *Children at Risk: In the Web of Parental Mental Illness,* New Brunswick: Rutgers University Press.

Fergusson, D.M., Horwood, l.J. and Lynskey, M.T. (1995) 'Maternal depressive symptoms and depressive symptoms in adolescents', *Journal of Child Psychology and Psychiatry,* Vol.36, No.7, pp.1161–1178.

Field, T., Healy, B., Goldstein, S. and Guthertz, M. (1990) 'Behaviour-state matching and synchrony in mother-infant interactions of nondepressed versus. depressed 'dyads', *Developmental Psychology,* Vol.26, pp.7–14.

Fombonne, E. (1995) 'Depressive disorders: time trends and possible explanatory mechanisms,' in Rutter, M. and Smith, D.J. (eds.) *Psycholosocial Disorders in Young People: Time Trends and Their Causes,* Chichester: Wiley.

Galloway, D.M., Ball, T., Blomfield, D. and Seyd, R. (1982) *Schools and Disruptive Behaviour,* London, Longman.

Gerada, C. (1996) 'The drug-addicted mother: pregnancy and lactation', in Gopfert, M., Webster, J. and Seeman, M.V. (eds.) *Parental Psychiatric Disorder: Distressed Parents and their Families,* Cambridge: Cambridge University Press.

Gibbons, J., Conroy, S. and Bell, C. (1995a) *Operating the Child Protection System: A study of child protection practices in English local authorities,* London, HMSO.

Gibbons, J., Gallagher, B., Bell, C. and Gordon, D. (1995b) *Development after Physical Abuse in Early Childhood,* London, HMSO.

Gibson, E. (1975) 'Homicide in England and Wales 1967–1971', *Home Office research study No. 31*, London, HMSO.

Glaser, D., Prior, V. and Lynch, M.A. (1997) *Emotional abuse: Suspicion, Investigation and Registration*, Unpublished report for the Department of Health.

Goodyer, I.M., Cooper, P.J., Vize, C.M. and Ashby, L. (1993) 'Depression in 11–16–year old girls: The role of past parental psychopathology and exposure to recent life events', *Journal of Child Psychology and Psychiatry*, Vol.34, pp.1103–15.

Gough, D. (1993) *Child Abuse Interventions: A Review of the Research Literature,* London: HMSO.

Graham, P., Rawlings, E. and Rimini, W. (1988) 'Survivors of terror: Battered women, hostages and the Stockholm syndrome', in Yllo, K. and Bograd, M. (eds) *Feminist Perspectives on Wife Abuse*, London: Sage.

Gray, J. (1993) 'Coping with unhappy children who exhibit emotional and behaviour problems in the classroom', in Varma, V. (ed) *Coping with Unhappy Children*, London: Cassell.

Greco-Vigorito, C., Drucker, P.M., Moore-Russell, M. and Avaltroni, J. (1996) 'Affective symptoms in young children of substance abusers correlate with parental distress', *Psychological Reports*, Vol.79, No.2, pp.547–552.

Greenwich Asian Women's Project (1996) *Annual Report*, London: Greenwich Asian Women's Project.

Hague, G. and Malos, E. (1994) 'Children, domestic violence and housing; the impact of homelessness', in Mullender, A. and Morley, R. (eds.) *Children Living with Domestic Violence*, Bournemouth: Whiting and Birch.

Hammen, C. (1988) 'Self cognitions, stressful events and the prediction of depression in children of depressed mothers', *Journal of Abnormal Child Psychology*, Vol.16, pp.347–60.

Hammen, C., Gordon, D., Burge, D., Adrian, C., Jaenicke, C. and Hiroto, G. (1978) 'Communication patterns of mothers with affective disorders and their relationship to children's status and social functioning', in Hahlweg, K. and Goldstein, M.J. (eds.) *Understanding major mental disorder: The contribution of family interaction research*, New York: Family Process Press.

Hamner, J. (1989) 'Women and policing in Britain', in Hamner, J., Radford, J. and Stanko, E.A. (eds.) *Women, Policing and Male Violence: International Perspectives*, London: Routledge.

Hardiker, P., Exton, K. and Barker, M. (1991) *Policies and practices in preventive child care*, Aldershot: Gower.

Hartup, W.W. (1983) 'Peer relations', in Mussen, P.H. (ed.) *Handbook of Child Psychology*, 4, pp.103–196, New York: Wiley.

Health Education Authority (1992) *Tomorrow's young adult: 9–15 year-olds look at alcohol, drugs, exercise and smoking*, London: H.E.A.

Herjanic, B.M., Barrido, V.H., Herjanic, M. and Tomeller, C.J. (1979) 'Children of heroin addicts', *The International Journal of the Addictions*, Vol.14, No.7, pp.919–931.

Herman, J.L. Perry, C. and van der Kolk, B. (1989) 'Childhood trauma in borderline personality disorder', *American Journal of Psychiatry*, Vol.146, pp.490–495.

Hester, M. and Radford, L (1995) 'Safety matters! Domestic violence and child contact, towards an inter-disciplinary response', *Representing Children*, Vol.8, No.4, pp.49–60.

Hester, M. and Radford, L. (1996) *Domestic Violence and Child Contact Arrangements in England and Denmark*, University of Bristol: Policy Press.

Hetherington, E., Cox, M. and Cox, R. (1978) 'The aftermath of divorce', in Stevens, J.H. and Matthews, M. (eds.) *Mother-Child, Father-Child Relations*, Washington DC: National Association for the Education of Young Children.

Hill, M., Leybourn, A. and Brown, J. (1996) 'Children whose parents misuse alcohol: a study of services and needs', *Child and Family Social Work*, Vol.1, No.3, pp.159–167.

Hodge, G.M., McCormick, J. and Elliott, R. (1997) 'Examination-induced distress in a public examination at the completion of secondary schooling', *British Journal of Educational Psychology*, Vol.67, No.2, pp.185–198.

Hoff, L.A. (1990) *Battered Women as Survivors*, London: Routledge.

Hogan, D.M. (1998) 'The psychological development and welfare of children of opiate and cocaine users: review and research needs', *Journal of Child Psychology and Psychiatry*, Vol.39, No.5, pp.609–620.

Holden, G.W. and Ritchie, K.L. (1991) 'Linking extreme marital discord, child rearing and child behaviour problems: evidence from battered women', *Child Development*, Vol.62, pp.311–27.

Home Office, (1994) *Criminal Statistics for England and Wales 1993*, Cm 2680, London: HMSO.

House of Commons (1991) *Lord President's Report on Action Against Alcohol Misuse*, London: HMSO.

Howe, D. (1995) *Attachment Theory for Social Work Practice*, London: Macmillan.

Hughes, H.M. (1988) 'Psychological and behavioural correlates of family violence in child witnesses and victims', *American Journal of Orthopsychiatry*, Vol.58, No.1, pp.77–90.

Hunt, J., Macleod, A., Thomas, C. and Freeman, P. (in press), *The last resort: Child protection, the courts and the 1989 Children Act*, London: HMSO.

Hyton, C. (1997) *Black families' survival strategies: ways of coping*, York: Joseph Rowntree Foundation.

Jaffe, P., Hurley, D.J. and Wolfe, D. (1990) 'Children's observations of violence: I. Critical issues in child development and intervention planning', *Canadian Journal of Psychiatry*, Vol.36, pp.466–470.

Jaffe, P., Wolfe, D. and Wilson, S. (1990) *Children of Battered Women*, London: Sage.

James, G. (1994) *Department of Health Discussion Report for ACPC Conference: Study of Working Together "Part 8" Reports*.

Jenkins, J.M. and Smith, M.A. (1990) 'Factors protecting children living in disharmonious homes: Maternal reports', *J. Am. Acad., Child Adolescent Psychiatry*, Vol.29, No.1, pp.60–69.

Johnson, M.A. and Johnson, F.D. (eds.) (1993) *HIV Infection in Women*, Churchill Livingstone, U.K.

Jones, D., Bentovim, A., Cameron, H., Vizard, E. and Wolkind, S. (1991) 'Signficant harm in context: the child psychiatrist's contribution', in Adcock, M., White, R. and Hollows, A. (eds) *Significant Harm*, Croydon: Significant Publications.

Joseph Rowntree Foundation (1996) *Domestic violence and child contact arrangements*, Social Policy Research, 100, York: Joseph Rowntree Foundation.

Juliana, P. and Goodman, C. (1997) 'Children of substance abusing parents', in Lowinson, J.H. (ed.), *Substance Abuse: A Comprehensive Textbook*, Baltimore: Williams and Wilkins.

Julien, R.M. (1995) *A Primer of Drug Action*, 7th Edition, New York: W.H. Freeman and Co.

Kandal, E.R., Schwartz, J.H. and Jessell, T.M. (1991) *Principles of Neural Science*, third edition, London: Prentice-Hall International (UK) Limited.

Karr, M. (1995) *The Liars' Club*, Harmondsworth: Penguin.

Kelleher and Associates and Monica O'Connor (1995) 'Making the links: Towards an integrated strategy for the elimination of violence against women in intimate relationships with men', quoted in Office of the Tanaiste, (1997) *Report of the Task Force on Violence against Women*, Dublin: Dublin.Stationery Office.

Kelly, L. (1988) *Surviving Sexual Violence*, Cambridge: Polity Press.

Kelly, L. (1994) 'The interconnectedness of domestic violence and child abuse: challenges for research policy and practice', in Mullender, A. and Morley, R. (eds.) *Children Living with Domestic Violence: Putting Men's Abuse of Women on the Child Care Agenda*, London: Whiting and Birch.

Kirkwood, C. (1993) *Leaving Abusive Partners: From the Scars of Survival to the Wisdom for Change*, London: Sage.

Klein, D., Clark, D., Dansky, L. and Margolis, E.T. (1988) 'Dysthymia in the offspring of parents with primary unipolar affective disorder', *Journal of Abnormal Psychology*, Vol.94, pp.1155–1127.

Kosonen, M. (1996) 'Siblings as providers of support and care during middle childhood: Children's perceptions', *Children and Society*, Vol.10, No.4, pp.267–279.

Lang, C., Field, T., Pickens, J., Martinez, A., Bendell, D., Yando, R., and Routh, D. (1996) 'Preschoolers of dysphoric mothers', *The Journal of Child Psychology and Psychiatry*, Vol.37, No.2, pp.221–224.

Langley, P. (1991) 'Family violence: Towards family oriented public policy', *Families in Society*, Vol.73, pp.574–576.

Lee, C.M. and Gotlib, I.H. (1989) 'Maternal depression and child adjustment: a longitudinal analysis', *Journal of Abnormal Psychology*, Vol.98, pp.78–85.

Leffert, N. and Petersen, A.C. (1995) 'Patterns of development in adolescence', in Rutter, M. and Smith, D.J. (eds.) *Psycho-social Disorders in Young People: Time Trends and their Causes*, Chichester: Wiley

Leitner, M., Shapland, J. and Wiles, P. (1993) *Drug usage and drugs prevention: The view and habits of the general public*, London: HMSO.

Leslie, B. (1993) 'Casework and client characteristics of cocaine crack using parents in a child welfare setting', *The Journal of The Ontario Association of Children's Aid Societies.*

Lewis, C.E. and Bucholz, K.K. (1991) 'Alcoholism, antisocial behaviour and family history', *British Journal of Addiction*, Vol.86, pp.177–194.

Littlewood, R. and Lipsedge, M. (1989) *Aliens and alienists: Ethnic minorities and psychiatry* (Second Edition), London: Routledge.

Lynskey, M.T., Fergusson, D.M. and Horwood, L.J. (1998) 'The origins of the correlations between tobacco, alcohol, and cannabis use during adolescence', *Journal of Child Psychology and Psychiatry*, Vol.39, No.7, pp.995–1006.

Maidment, S. (1976) 'A study in child custody', *Family Law*, Vol.6, pp.195–200, pp.236–41.

Maitra, B. (1995) 'Giving due consideration to the family's racial and cultural background', in Reder, P. and Lucey, C. (eds.) *Assessment of parenting: Psychiatric and psychological contributions*, London: Routledge.

Malos, E. and Hague, G. (1997) 'Women, Housing, Homelessness and Domestic Violence', *Women's Studies International Forum*, Vol.20, No.3.

Mayhew, P., Maung, N.A. and Mirrlees-Black, C. (1993) *The 1992 British Crime Survey*, Home Office Research Study No132, London: HMSO.

McGee, C. (1996) *Children's and Mother's Experiences of Child Protection Following Domestic Violence*, A paper given at the Brighton Conference, Violence, Abuse and Women's Citizenship International Conference.

McWilliams, M. and McKiernan, J. (1993) *Bringing it out in the Open – Domestic Violence in Northern Ireland.*

Merikangas, K., Dierker, L.C. and Szatmari (1998) Psychopathology among offspring of parents with substance abuse and/or anxiety disorders: a high-risk study', *Journal of Child Psychology and Psychiatry*, Vol.39, No.5, pp.711–720.

Merikangas, K. and Spiker, D.G. (1982) 'Assortative mating among in-patients with primary affective disorder', *Psychological Medicine*, Vol.212, pp.753–764.

Merikangas, K., Weissman, M. Prusoff B. and John, K. (1998) 'Assortative mating and affective disorders: Psychopathology in offspring', *Psychiatry*, Vol.51, pp.48–57.

Milne, A.A. (1971) *Now we are Six*, London: Methuen.

Moffitt, T.E. (1993) Adolescent-limited and life-course-persistent anti-social behavior: A developmental taxonomy, *Psychological Review*, Vol.4, pp.674–701.

Moffitt, T.E. and Caspi, A. (1998) 'Implications of violence between intimate partners for child psychologists and psychiatrists', *Journal of Child Psychology and Psychiatry*, Vol.39, No.2, pp.137–144.

Monck E., Bentovin, A., Goodall, G., Hyde, C., Lwin, R., Sharland, E. with Elton, A. (1996) *Child Sexual Abuse: A Descriptive and Treatment Study*, London: HMSO.

Monck, E. and New, M. (1996) *Report of a Study of Sexually Abused Children and Adolescents, and of Young Perpetrators of Sexual Abuse Who Were Treated in Voluntary Agency Community Facilities*, London: HMSO.

Mooney, J. (1994) *The Hidden Figure: Domestic Violence in North London*, London: Islington Council.

Morley, R. and Mullender, A. (1994) 'Domestic violence and children: What do we know from research', in Mullender, A. and Morley, R. (eds.) *Children Living With Domestic Violence: Putting Men's Abuse of Women on the Child Care Agenda*, London: Whiting and Birch Ltd.

Mullender, A., Debbonaire, T., Hauge, G., Kelly, L. and Malos, E. (1998) 'Working with children in women's refuges', *Children and Family Social Work*, Vol.3, No.2, pp.87–98.

Murray, L. (1992) 'The impact of postnatal depression on infant development,' *Journal of Child Psychology and Psychiatry*, Vol.33, pp.543–561.

Murray, L., Hipwell, A. and Hooper, R., Stein, A. and Cooper (1996) 'The cognitive development of 5–year-old children of postnatally depressed mothers', *Journal of Child Psychology and Psychiatry*, Vol.37, No.8, pp.927–935.

National Institute on Alcohol Abuse and Alcoholism (1990) Children of Alcoholics: Are they different? *NIAAA Alcohol Alert No. 9*, internet web site http://www.drugs.indiana.edu/radar/alerts/alert9.html, July 1997.

NCH Action For Children (1994) *The Hidden Victims: Children and Domestic Violence*, London: NCH Action For Children.

Norton, K. and Dolan, B. (1996) 'Personality disorder and parenting', in Gopfert, M., Webster, J. and Seeman, M.V. (eds) *Parental Psychiatric Disorder: Distressed parents and their families*, Cambridge: Cambridge University Press.

NSPCC, (1997a) *Long Term Problems, Short Term Solutions: Parents in Contact with Mental Health Services*, Brent: Brent. ACPC.

NSPCC (1997b) 'Drunk in Charge: Substance Abuse', *Community Care*, 11–17 September, p.35.

Office of Population and Censuses and Surveys (1995) *Smoking Amongst Secondary School Children in 1994.*, London: HMSO.

Office of Population and Censuses and Surveys (1996) *The prevalance of psychiatric morbidity among adults living in private households*, London: HMSO.

Office of the Tanaiste (1997) *Report of the Task Force on Violence Against Women*, Dublin: Stationery Office.

O'Hara, M.W., Neunaber, D.J. and Zekoski, E.M. (1984) 'Prospective study of postpartum depression: Prevalence, course and predictive factors', *Journal of Abnormal Psychology*, Vol.93, pp.158–171.

Orford, J. and Velleman, R. (1990) 'Offspring of parents with drinking problems: drinking and drug-taking as young adults', *British Journal of Addiction*, Vol.85, pp.779–794.

Owusu-Bempah, J. (1995) 'Information about the absent parent as a factor in the well-being of children of single-parent families', *International Social Work*, Vol.38, pp.253–275.

Owusu-Bempah and Howitt, J. (1997) 'Self-identity and black children in care', in Davies, M. (ed.) *The Blackwell Companion to Social Work*, London: Blackwell.

Packman, J. and Hall, C. (1998) *From Care to Accommodation,* London: HMSO.

Pahl, J. (1985) *Private Violence and Public Policy*, London: Routledge and Kegan Paul.

Panaccione, V. and Wahler, R. (1986) 'Child behaviour, maternal depression, and social coercion as factors in the quality of child care', *Journal of Abnormal Child Psychology*, Vol.14, pp.273–284.

Pence, E. and McMahon, M. (1998) 'Duleth: A co-ordinated community response to domestic violence', in Harwin, N., Hague, G. and Malos, E. (eds) *Domestic Violence and Multi-Agency Working: New Opportunities, Old Challenges*, London: Whiting and Birch.

Plant, M. (1985) *Drinking and Pregnancy*, London: Tavistock Publications.

Plant, M. (1997) *Women and Alcohol: Contemporary and Historical Perspectives*, London: Free Association Books.

Post, F. (1962) 'The social orbit of psychiatric patients', *J. Ment. Sci.*, Vol.108, p.759.

Pound, A., Cox, A.D., Puckering, C. and Mills, M. (1984) 'Do depressed women have an identifiable parenting style?', in Stevenson, J. (ed.) *Recent Research in Developmental Psychopathology*, Oxford: Pergamon.

Pound, A., Puckering, C., Mills, M. and Cox, A.D. (1988) 'The impact of maternal depression on young children', *British Journal of Psychotherapy*, Vol.4, pp.240–252.

Quinton, D. and Rutter, M. (1985) 'Family pathology and child psychiatric disorder: A four-year prospective study', in: Nicol, A.R. (ed) *Longitudinal Studies in Child Psychology and Psychiatry*, London: John Wiley and Sons Ltd.

Rack, P. (1982) *Race, Culture and menatl Disorder*, London: Tavistock.

Radke-Yarrow, M., Cummings, E.M., Kueznski, L. and Chapman, M. (1985) 'Patterns of attachment in two and three year olds in normal families and families with parental depression', *Child Development*, Vol.56, No.4, pp.884–93.

Radke-Yarrow, M., Richters, J. and Wilson, W.E. (1988) 'Child development in a network of relationships', in Hinde, R.A. and Stevenson-Hinde, J. (eds) *Relations Within Families, Mutual Influences.*, Oxford: Oxford University Press.

Ramsey, M. and Spiller, J. (1997) *Drug Misuse Declared in 1996: Key Results from the British Crime Survey*, Research Findings No. 56, Home Office Research and Statistics Directorate, London: Home Office.

Reading, A. (1983) *Psychological Aspects of Pregnancy*, London: Longman.

Reder, P. and Duncan, S. (1997) 'Adult Psychiatry – A missing link in the child protection network: Comments on Falkow's 'Fatal child abuse and parental psychiatric disorder' (DOH, 1996)', *Child Abuse Review*, Vol.6, pp.35–40.

Report of the Committee on Local Authority and Allied Personal Social Services (Seebohm) *CMND 3703*, HMSO, 1968.

Resnich, P.J. (1969) 'Child murder by parents: A psychiatric review of filicide', *Amer. J. Psychiat.*, Vol.126, pp.325–334.

Resti, M., Azzaro. C., Mannelli, F., Moriondo, M., Novembre, E., de Martino, M., Vieruci, A. and Tuscany Study Group on Hepatitis C Virus Infection in Children (1998) 'Mother to child transmission of hepatitits C virus: prospective study of risk factors and timing of infection in children born to women seronegative for HIV-1', *British Medical Journal*, Vol.317, pp.437–440.

Richman, N., Stevenson, J. and Harris, T. (1982) *Pre-school to school: A Behavioural Study*, London: Academic Press.

Rickford, F. (1996) Bad Habit, *Community Care*, 1–14 February.

Riley, J.W. (1920) *Riley Child-Rhymes*, New York: Bobbs-Merrill.

Rivinus, T.M. (1991) *Children of Chemically Dependent Parents*, New York: Drunner/Mazel Publishers.

Rosett, H.L. (1980) 'The effects of alcohol on the foetus and offspring', in Kalant, O.J. (ed.) *Alcohol and Drug Problems in Women: Research Advances in Alcohol and Drug Problems*, 5, pp.595–645, New York: Plenum Press.

Ross, E.M. (1996) 'Risk of abuse to children of spouse abusing parents', *Child Abuse and Neglect*, Vol.20, No.7, pp.589–598.

Rowbottom, R., Hey, A. and Billis, D. (1974) *Social Services Departments, Developing Patterns of Work and Organization*, London: Heinemann Educational Books.

Royal College of General Practitioners (1996) *The Health of Adolescents in Primary Care: How to Promote Adolescent Health in Your Practice,* London: Royal College of General Practitioners.

Royal College of Physicians (1991) *Alcohol and the Public Health,* London: Macmillan Education.

Royal College of Physicians (1995) *Alcohol and the young,* London: Royal Lavenham Press.

Rubio-Stipec, M., Bird, H., Canino, M., Bravo, M. and Alegeri, M. (1991) 'Children of alcoholic parents in the community', *Journal of Studies on Alcohol,* Vol.52, No.1, pp.78–88.

Rutter, M. (1966) *Children of Sick Parents: An Environmental and Psychiatric Study,* Institute of Psychiatry Maudsley Monographs No. 16, Oxford: Oxford University Press.

Rutter, M, (1985) 'Resilience in the face of adversity. Protective factors and resistance to psychiatric disorder', *British Journal of Psychiatry ,* Vol.147, pp.598–611.

Rutter, M. (1989) 'Psychiatric disorder in parents as a risk factor for children', in Schaffer, D. (ed) *Prevention of Mental Disorder, alcohol and other drug use in children and adolescents,* Rockville, Md: Office for Substance Abuse, USDHHS.

Rutter, M. (1990) 'Commentary: some focus and process considerations regarding effects of parental depression on children', *Developmental Psychology,* Vol.26, pp.60–67.

Rutter, M. (1995) Clinical implications of Attachment Concepts: Retrospect and Prospect, *Journal of Child Psychology and Psychiatry,* Vol.36, No.4, pp.549–571.

Rutter, M., Graham, P., Chadwick, O, and Yule, W. (1976) 'Adolescent turmoil: fact or fiction', *Journal of Child Psychology and Psychiatry,* Vol.17, pp. 35–56.

Rutter, M. and Quinton, D. (1984) 'Parental psychiatric disorder: Effects on children', *Psychological Medicine,* Vol.14, pp.853–880.

Rutter M. and Rutter, M. (1992) *Developing Minds: Challenge and Continuity across the Life Span,* Harmondsworth: Penguin.

Rydelius, P.A. (19970 'Are children of alcoholics a clinical concern for child and adolescent psychiatrists of today?' *The Journal of Child Psychology and Psychiatry,* Vol.38, No.6, pp.615–624.

Saunders, A. (1994) 'Children in women's refuges: A retrospective study', in Mullender, A. and Morley, R. (eds.) *Children Living With Domestic Violence: Putting Men's Abuse of Women on the Child Care Agenda*, London: Whiting and Birch Ltd.

Saunders, A., Keep, A. and Debbonaire, T. (1995) *It Hurts me Too: Children's Experiences of Domestic Violence and Refuge Life*, London: Women's Aid Federation England (WAFE), National Institute for Social Work, (NISW) and ChildLine.

Sharland, E., Seal, H., Croucher, M., Aldgate, J. and Jones, D. (1996) *Professional Intervention in Child Sexual Abuse*, London: HMSO.

Sharp, D., Hay, D.F., Pawlby, S., Schmucker, G., Allen, H. and Kumar, R. (1995) 'The impact of postnatal depression on boys' intellectual development', *The Journal of Child Psychology and Psychiatry*, Vol.36, No.8, pp.1315–1336.

Sheppard, M. (1993) 'Maternal depression and child care: the significance for social work and social work research', *Adoption and Fostering*, Vol.17, No.2, pp.10–15.

Sheppard, M. (1997) 'Double jeopardy: The link between child abuse and maternal depression in child and family social work', *Child and Family Social Work*, Vol.2, No.2, pp.91–108.

Skuse, D., Stevenson, P., Hodges, J., et al (1997) *The Influence of Early Experience of Sexual Abuse on the Formation of Sexual Preferences During Adolescence*, London: Institute of Child Health.

Skuse, D., Bentovim, A., Hodges, J., Stevenson, J., Andreou, C., Lanyado, M., New, M., Williams, B. and McMillan, D. (1998) 'Risk factors for development of sexually abusive behaviour in sexually victimised adolescent boys: cross sectional study', *British Medical Journal*, No.317, pp.175–179.

Smith P.K. and Cowie, H. (1991) *Understanding Children's Development*, Oxford: Blackwell.

Smith, P.K. and Thompson (1991) 'Dealing with bully/victim problems in the UK', in Smith, P.K. and Thompson, D. (eds.) *Practical Approaches to Bullying*, London: David Fulton.

Spieker, S.J. and Booth, C. (1988) 'Family risk typologies and patterns of insecure attachment', in Belsky, J. and Nezworski, T. (eds.) *Clinical implications of attachment*, Hillsdale, pp.95–135, NJ.: Erlbaum.

Stafford, E.M., Jackson, P.R. and Banks, M.H. (1980) 'Employment, work involvement and mental health in less qualified young people', *Journal of Occupational Psychology*, Vol.53, pp.291–304.

Standing Conference on Drug Abuse (1997) *Drug using parents: policy guidelines for inter-agency working*, London: Local Government Association.

Stark, E. and Flitchcraft, A. and Frazier, W. (1979) 'Medicine and Patriarchal Violence: The Social Construction of a Private Event', *International Journal of Health Services*, Vol.9, No.3, pp.461–493.

Statistics Canada (1993) *The Violence Against Women Survey*, Centre for Justice Statistics.

Stewart, M.A., Deblois, C.S. and Cummings, C. (1980) 'Psychiatric disorder in the parents of hyperactive boys and those with conduct disorder', *Journal of Child Psychology and Psychiatry*, Vol.21, pp.283–292.

Stocker, C.M. (1994) 'Children's perceptions of relationships with siblings, friends, and mothers: compensatory processes and links with adjustment', *Journal of Child Psychology and Psychiatry*, Vol.15, No.8, pp.1447–1459.

Stott, D.H. (1973) Follow-up study from birth of the effects of pre-natal stresses, *Am. J. Psychiat.* Vol.118, pp.781–794.

Stroud, J. (1997) 'Mental disorder and the homicide of children', *Social Work and Social Sciences Review: An International Journal of Applied Research* , Vol.6, No.3, 1996–97, pp.149–162.

Svedin, C.G., Wadsby, M. and Sydsjo, G (1996) 'Children of mothers who are at psycho-social risk: Mental health, behaviour problems and incidence of child abuse at age 8 years', *European Child and Adolescent Psychiatry* , Vol. 5, pp.162–171.

Swadi, H. (1994) 'Parenting capacity and substance misuse: An assessment scheme', *ACPP Review and Newsletter,* Vol.16, No.5, pp. 237–244.

Thoburn, J. (1996) 'Psychological parenting and child placement: 'But we want to have our cake and eat it', in Howe, D. (ed.) *Attachment and Loss in Child and Family Social Work*, Aldershot: Avebury.

Thoburn, J., Lewis, A. and Shemmings, D. (1995) *Paternalism or Partnership? Family Involvement in the Child Protection Process,* London: HMSO.

Thoburn, J., Wilding, J. and Watson, J. (forthcoming) *Family Support in Cases of Emotional Maltreatment and Neglect*.

Thomas, A. and Niner, P. (1989) *Living in Temporary Accommodation: A Survey of Homeless People*, London: London Press.

Toolis, K. (1998) *Of Human Darkness*, The Guardian Weekend, January 17.

Torgersen, S. (1983) 'Genetics of neurosis: the effects of sampling variation upon the twin concordance ratio', *British Journal of Psychiatry*, Vol.142, pp.126–132.

Trent Drug Misuse Database (1998) *Drug Misuse Database*, Leicester: Drury House.

Tunstill, J., and Aldgate, J. (forthcoming) *Family Support: From Policy to Practice*, Stationery Office.

Tweed, S.H. (1991) 'Adult children of alcoholics: Profiles of wellness amidst distress', *Journal of Studies on Alcohol*, Vol.52, No.2, pp.133–141.

van Beek, I., Dwyer, R., Dore, G.J., Luo, K, and Kaldor, J.M. (1998) 'Infection with HIV and hepatitis C virus among injecting drug users in a prevention setting: retrospective cohort study', *British Medical Journal*, Vol.317, pp.433–437.

Velleman, R. (1993) *Alcohol and the Family*, Institute of Alcohol Studies.

Velleman, R. (1996) 'Alcohol and drug problems in parents: an overview of the impact on children and the implications for practice', in Gopfert, M. Webster, J. and Seeman, M.V. (eds.) *Parental Psychiatric Disorder: Distressed Parents and their Families*, Cambridge: Cambridge University Press.

Velleman, R. and Orford, J. (1993) 'The importance of family discord in explaining childhood problems', *Addiction Research*, Vol.1, No.1, pp.39–57.

Wade, J. and Biehal, N. with Clayden, J. and Stein, M. (1998) *Going Missing: Young People Absent from Care*, Report to the Department of Health.

Walker, F. (1995) *Young people and alcohol*, Highlight No 138, London: National Children's Bureau.

Ward, H. (1995) (ed) *Looking After Children: Research into Practice*, London: HMSO.

Warr, P.B., Banks, M.H. and Ullah, P. (1985) 'The experience of unemployment among black and white urban teenagers', *British Journal of Psychology*, Vol.76, pp.75–87.

Weissman, M.M. John, K., Merikangas, K.R., Prusoff, B.A., Wickramaratne, P., Gammon, G.D., Angold, A. and Warner, V. (1986) 'Depressed parents and their children: General health, social and psychiatric problems', *American Journal of Diseases of Children*, Vol.140, pp.801–805.

Weissman, M.M. and Paykel, E.S. (1974) *The Depressed Woman: A Study of Social Relationships*, Chicago: University of Chicago Press.

Weissman, M.M., Paykel, E.S. and Klerman, F.L. (1972) 'The depressed woman as a mother', *Social Psychiatry*, Vol.7, pp.98–108.

Weissman, M.M., Prusoff, B.A., Gammon, G.D., Merikangas, K.R., Leckman, J.F. and Kidd, K.K. (1984) 'Psychopathology of the children (ages 6–18) of depressed and normal parents', *Journal of the American Academy of Child Psychiatry* , Vol.23, pp.78–84

Werner, E.E. (1986) 'Resilient offspring of alcoholics: A longitudinal study from birth to age 18', *Journal of Studies on Alcohol*, Vol.47, No.1, pp.34–40.

West, M.O. and Prinz, R.J. (1987) 'Parental alcoholism and childhood psychopatholgy', *Psychological Bulletin*, Vol.102, No.2, pp.204–218.

Western, D., Ludolph, P., Misle, B. et al. (1990) Physical and sexual abuse in adolescent girls with borderline personality disorder, *American Journal of Orthopsychiatry*, Vol.60, pp. 55–66.

Wolfe, D.A., Jaffe, P., Wilson, S.K and Zak, L. (1985) 'Children of battered women: the relation of child behaviour to family violence and maternal stress', *Journal of Consulting and Clinical Psychology*, Vol.53, No.5, pp.657–665.

Wolkind, S. (1981) 'Pre-natal emotional stress – effects on the foetus', in Wolkind, S. and Zajicek, E. (eds.) *Pregnancy: A Psychological and Social Study*, London: Academic Press.

Women's Aid (1995) *Domestic violence, the social context*, Dublin: Womens Aid.

Women's Aid Federation England (1991) *Women's Aid Federation England Information Pack*, Bristol: WAFE.

Women's Aid Federation England (1993) *Evidence to the House of Commons Home Affairs Committee into Domestic Violence*, Bristol: WAFE.

Women's Aid Federation England (1997) *Women's Aid Federation England Annual Survey*, 1996–7, Bristol: WAFE.

World Health Organisation (1978) *Mental Disorders: Glossary and Guide to their Classification in Accordance with the Ninth Revision of the International Classification of Diseases* (ICD-9), Geneva: World Health Organisation.

World Health Organisation (1992) *The ICD-10 Classification of Mental and Behavioural Disorders*, Geneva: World Health Organisation.

Zimmerman, M. and Coryell, W.H. (1990) 'Diagnosing personality disorders in the community', *Archives of General Psychiatry*, Vol.47, pp.527–31.

Acknowledgements

We acknowledge with sincere thanks the many people who gave generously of their time to help us with this study. We particularly appreciate the expertise and advice offered by Arnon Bentovim, Richard Velleman, Panos Vostanis and Wendy Rose. The work has been funded by the Department of Health and we thank staff in the Department, particularly Jenny Gray who supported us throughout the study by her interest and valuable comments. We must also acknowledge the contribution made by Pam Freeman. Chris Cazalet gave willing and efficient secretarial support.

Advisory group members

Jenny Gray (Chair)
Department of Health
Wellington House
London

Ravinder Barn
Royal Holloway
University of London
Surrey

Arnon Bentovim
The London Child and Family
Consultation Service
234 Great Portland Street
London

Reba Bhaduri
Department of Health
Wellington House
London

Jim Brown
Department of Health
Wellington House
London

Paul Clark
Department of Health
Hannibal House
London

Carolyn Davies
Department of Health
405A Skipton House
London

Ruth Dixon
Social Services Department
Southampton City Council
Southampton

Bob Jezzard
Department of Health
Wellington House
London

Nicola Harwin
Women's Aid Federation
(England) Ltd.
Bristol

Lynne Hopkins
Director of Social Services
Bournemouth Borough Council
Bournemouth

Paul Johnson
Social Services Department
Bradford

Ilan Katz
NSPCC
National Centre
London

Arran Poyser
Department of Health
Wellington House
London

Ellen Malos
Research Officer
School of Policy Studies
University of Bristol

Marjorie Smith
Thomas Coram Research Unit
London

Adrian Falkov
Parkside House
Department of Child Psychiatry
London

Dr. Richard Velleman
Director, Research and
Development
Bath Mental Health Care

Local reference panel

Alex Coppello
Addictive Behaviour Unit
All Saints Hospital
Birmingham

Basem Farid
Consultant Psychiatrist
Leicestershire Mental Health

Debby Hindle
Psychotherapist
Child and Adolescent Psychiatry Unit
Nottingham

Sapphire Naylor
Alcohol and Drugs Unit
Nottingham

Sue Stokes
Child Care Team Manager
Social Services Department
Birmingham

Janet Seden
Lecturer
School of Social Work
Leicester University

Panos Vostanis
Professor of Child and Adolescent
Psychiatry
Geenwood Institute of Child Health
Leicester

Stephen Wells
Gelding Area Director
Social Services Department
Nottingham

Judy Worral
Alcohol Advice Centre
Leicester

Index

Page numbers in italics refer to tables and boxed material.